CONTENTS

INTRODUCTION

Butterball. The very sound of the word rolling off the tongue conjures images of juicy slices of tender turkey. Since 1954, Butterball has become synonymous with turkey, and a Thanksgiving staple. Indeed, generations of Americans across the country have continuously relied on this one brand of turkey for the most important, cherished meal of the year.

The name *Butterball* was chosen simply to connote a full, broad-breasted turkey—not because the turkeys contained butter, as some may believe. And through the years, it has been consumer input and changes in America's eating habits that have shaped the brand to become the national best-seller it is today.

From the beginning, Butterball set standards and employed innovative techniques unlike any other turkey company. For instance, the brand introduced the "bar strap" method of tucking the legs under the skin, which means no messy trussing, skewering, or awkward metal clips. And improved cleaning methods ensured that each turkey was free of pinfeathers.

In 1957, Butterball devised a system for removing most major leg tendons from the birds so that the drumsticks are easier to carve and eat. Offering cooks another helping hand in 1965, the company added an outside netting to protect the package from tearing or puncture and gave the consumer a handle for carrying the bird.

Reacting to consumer complaints of dry, overcooked turkey, in 1967 Butterball placed its patented Tendergold basting formula deep inside the white meat of frozen turkeys. Each turkey is individually weighed and the quantity of the vegetable-based formula placed in the breast is based on 3 percent of each turkey's body weight.

New, textured plastic bags were developed in 1971 so that consumers could easily remove the neck and giblets even if the turkey was still partially frozen. The next year Butterball introduced another patented invention: the Turkey Lifter. Each Butterball Turkey comes with this special string cradle, allowing cooks to lift the hot bird from the roasting pan and place it onto the platter safely, easily, and without marring the skin.

Butterball realized that in between holidays many people forget how to prepare and roast a turkey, so it began printing information folders to be included with each bird in 1975. These individually wrapped instructions cover the turkey preparation gamut from thawing, cooking, carving, and storing explanations to roasting schedules and recipes for such Thanksgiving fundamentals as giblet gravy and stuffing. Then, in 1981, Butterball opened its toll-free Turkey Talk-Line, designed to assist chefs struggling with the holiday bird. The Butterball Turkey Talk-Line was staffed then with four home economists who received eleven thousand phone calls. Today, the Talk-Line is considered *the authority* on turkey preparation and the staff of forty-four home economists expects more than two hundred seventy thousand calls each November and December.

Butterball continued to ruffle the feathers of its fowl competitors in 1985, and then again in 1987, by improving the basting process and formula. Uniform formula dispersion in the breast meat ensures every Butterball cook will slice into a premium, juicy, tender, and moist turkey. And Butterball has continued to expand the product lineup, demonstrating turkey is not just for Thanksgiving. The Butterball Turkey Company offers products and recipes for every meal occasion, whether the situation requires eating on the run or a more elegant, formal culinary delight. Butterball products are a feast for the eyes as well as the stomach and may be prepared in the oven, on the stove, in the microwave, or on the grill for a delicious and nutritious meal any time of year.

The people of the Butterball Turkey Company are proud of their heritage and diligently work to bring their customers the best products to fit today's life-styles. By directly consulting consumers, Butterball is consistently improving existing product lines and creating new ones based on suggestions from consumers on what they would like to see on the market. It is Butterball's aim to provide consumers with premium quality turkey products, recipes, and services, offering both new and long-time customers the opportunity to take advantage of the Butterball difference.

TURKEY TALK: EVERYTHING YOU NEED TO KNOW ABOUT TURKEY

No matter where we turn we are advised to eat more poultry. The ever-growing availability of turkey parts makes eating the all-American bird more appetizing and convenient than ever before. But as delicious, versatile, and practical as turkey is, its nutritional benefits make it a champion status, too.

For calorie counters, turkey is a superstar. The white meat has about half the fat of dark meat. A three-ounce serving of skinned breast meat has about 120 calories and only one to two grams of fat. Three ounces of skinned dark meat have about 145 calories and four to five grams of fat. Ground turkey contains about half of the fat found in lean ground beef, and turkey franks have about a third less fat than franks made from beef and pork.

All meat is a good source of protein and valuable vitamins and minerals. Turkey is especially high in niacin and vitamin B_6. Armed with the following recipes, you will have no trouble feeding your family healthful, delicious meals regardless of the season and, of more immediate concern, your busy schedule.

THE DIFFERENT SHAPES OF BUTTERBALL

Butterball sells turkey in all shapes and sizes. No longer are shoppers relegated to a big whole bird. Now, in supermarkets from coast to coast, you can buy fresh and frozen turkeys, smaller birds called Li'l Butterballs, already-stuffed frozen turkeys, fresh and frozen turkey breasts, boneless turkeys and turkey breasts, ground turkey, an assortment of turkey parts, and sausages and cold cuts. This way, regardless of the occasion or the size of your family, you can enjoy healthful, low-fat, good-tasting turkey anytime, anywhere.

We understand that having so many choices sometimes results in confusion, and so to make shopping for Butterball turkey easier than ever, we offer a quick-and-easy glossary of our products. Try them all, using the recipes that follow. You will discover you are getting more out of turkey than you ever imagined possible. And that's good news!

Butterball Turkey, Frozen and Fresh: These whole birds weigh from 9 to 24 pounds. Those heavier than 16 pounds generally are toms, while the smaller turkeys are hens. Both taste equally good and have the same proportion of white and dark meat. Whether frozen or fresh, most leg tendons have been removed for easier carving and the legs are tucked under a band of skin to eliminate the need for trussing. A handy Turkey Lifter is packed with each Butterball turkey.

Buying Guide: We suggest allowing 1 to 1½ pounds per person.

Li'l Butterball, Frozen and Fresh: These small whole birds weigh from 4 to 9 pounds and so are ideal for small families and for microwave cooking and barbecuing. When you buy a Li'l Butterball, you also get a special patented Turkey Lifter, an 8-ounce gravy packet, and giblets.

Buying Guide: We suggest allowing 1 to 1½ pounds per person.

Butterball Frozen Stuffed Turkey: These are incredibly convenient as they come already stuffed with an old-fashioned bread stuffing. What is more, they must go directly from the freezer to the oven with *no thawing*! This makes them just right for first-time or nervous turkey cooks, and anyone pressed for time. All our prestuffed birds are frozen and weigh from 6 to 16 pounds. A Turkey Lifter comes with each Butterball Turkey.

Buying Guide: We suggest allowing 1½ to 2 pounds per person.

Butterball Breast of Turkey, Frozen and Fresh: When all you want is white meat, consider a fresh or frozen breast. With the bone in, you can stuff the breast with your favorite dressing, if you choose. These weigh from 3 to 9 pounds.

Buying Guide: We suggest allowing ¾ of a pound per person.

Butterball Boneless Turkey, Frozen and Fresh: With these, you get all the meat, white and dark, without the bones. The boneless turkeys weigh 3 pounds. Frozen boneless turkeys are packaged with an 8-ounce gravy packet.

Buying Guide: We suggest allowing ½ pound per person.

Butterball Boneless Breast of Turkey, Frozen and Fresh: For white meat lovers, these convenient breasts are a breeze to cook and serve. The boneless breast weighs 3 pounds. The frozen breast comes with an 8-ounce gravy packet.

Buying Guide: We suggest allowing ½ pound per person.

Butterball Fresh Premium Turkey Cuts: These are ideal for grilling in the summertime and for light and easy meals anytime. Once you begin cooking with turkey cuts you will find them amazingly convenient and versatile. Following is a list of the numerous premium cuts available in the supermarkets, with the average ounce weight of each package. All are made from white meat, which clearly is America's favorite.

Butterball Turkey Breast Strips: 1.2 pounds average package weight

Butterball Boneless Turkey Breast Cutlets: 6 pieces per package; 1.2 pounds average package weight

Butterball Turkey Breast Chops: 3 to 4 fresh pieces per package; 1 pound average package weight

Butterball Turkey Breast Medallions: 1.2 pounds average package weight

Butterball Boneless Turkey Breast Roast: ½ breast per package; 1.5 pounds average package weight

Butterball Ground Turkey: Ground turkey is as versatile as any ground meat and far more good for you. Cooked ground turkey contains about one quarter the amount of fat as cooked lean ground beef. Make turkey patties, turkey meat loaf, turkey meatballs, turkey casseroles. The list goes on and on.

Butterball Cold Cuts: We make a complete line of poultry cold cuts in a wide array of sizes and varieties, perfect for sandwiches and quick snacks. Our cold cuts are up to 98 percent fat-free.

Butterball Slice 'N Serve: For quick, nutritious meals, try this fully cooked turkey breast. As the name suggests, all you do is "slice and serve"—what could be easier? Our Slice 'N Serve turkeys are up to 96 percent fat-free and are available Oven Prepared, Hickory Smoked, and Honey Roasted.

Buying Guide: We suggest allowing ¼ pound per person.

Butterball Turkey Franks and Butterball Turkey Smoked Sausage: Both our franks and smoked sausages are made from naturally lean turkey, are fully cooked, and taste great. Turkey franks are 80 percent fat-free and turkey smoked sausage is 90 percent fat-free.

THE RIGHT WAY TO STORE TURKEY

Cooked or uncooked, fresh or frozen, turkey should be stored with care. Never leave thawed, uncooked turkey or any poultry at room temperature. It may spoil in a matter of hours, depending on the heat of the day and the kitchen. Cooked turkey is also susceptible to bacterial growth at room temperature and should be refrigerated within an hour or two after the meal.

Frozen turkeys keep in the freezer for months, and even after a year are safe to eat (they may lose some flavor, however). Turkeys frozen for as long as seven months taste as good as fresh.

When dealing with fresh or frozen turkey, use your common sense and follow our guidelines for optimal safety.

Fresh Uncooked Turkey: Keep fresh turkey in the unopened wrapper in the refrigerator at 40° F. or below. Remember that in most refrigerators the lower shelves and the back of the box are the coldest areas. Cook the bird within 2 to 4 days after purchase—the USDA recommends waiting no longer than 2 days to cook fresh poultry. Birds kept in the coldest part of the refrigerator are satisfactory after 4 days.

Frozen Uncooked Turkey: Leave frozen turkey in its unopened wrapper and stow it in a zero-degree or lower freezer. For maximum flavor, thaw and cook the bird within 6 to 7 months.

Thawed Uncooked Turkey: Keep thawed turkey in the unopened wrapper in the refrigerator and use it within 2 to 4 days. Because the texture may be impaired, we do not recommend refreezing the bird, but if for some reason you must and if the turkey has been properly thawed (page 7) and refrigerated for no longer than 2 days, food safety is not a problem. For best results, the bird should still feel cold and preferably have some ice crystals clinging to it. Refreeze the turkey in its original wrapper, or if it is torn, overwrap it.

Cooked Turkey and Stuffing: Remove the stuffing from the bird's cavity within 2 hours after roasting, which usually means directly after the meal. Promptly refrigerate or freeze both the turkey and the stuffing separately. Eat refrigerated turkey and stuffing within 3 days; eat frozen stuffing within a month of freezing and frozen cooked turkey within 2 months of freezing.

THE RIGHT WAY TO THAW FROZEN TURKEY

There are two acceptable ways to thaw frozen turkey. One is the refrigerator method and the other is the cold-water method. The absolute *wrong* way to thaw turkey is to leave it at room temperature on the kitchen counter. Temperatures between 40 and 140°F. invite more rapid spoilage. The important thing to remember is to keep the bird cold during thawing.

Refrigerator Method: This is the preferred method of thawing, primarily because it is easiest and most foolproof. Place the still-wrapped turkey, breast up, on a shallow tray and slide it onto a refrigerator shelf. The tray, which may be any rimmed, flat pan such as a jelly-roll or roasting pan, catches juices that may leak from the wrapper as the bird thaws. The chart below indicates how many 24-hour days are required to thaw different-sized turkeys in the refrigerator at 40°F.

Cold-Water Method: If time is an issue, frozen turkey thaws very nicely when submerged in cold water. Place the turkey in the unopened wrapper, breast down, in enough cold water to cover. This may be a filled sink, if you can spare the space, or a large pot or tub. Change the water every 30 minutes to keep it good and cold. The chart below indicates how many hours are required to thaw different-sized turkeys by submerging in cold water.

THAWING TIMES FOR TURKEY

(Do not thaw Butterball Stuffed Turkey)

	Refrigerator Method	Cold-Water Method
Li'l Butterball	1½ to 2 days	3 to 4 hours
Whole turkey		
9 to 12 pounds	1½ to 2 days	4 to 6 hours
12 to 16 pounds	2 to 3 days	6 to 9 hours
16 to 20 pounds	3 to 4 days	9 to 11 hours
20 to 24 pounds	4 to 5 days	11 to 12 hours
Breast of turkey	1 to 2 days	4 to 8 hours
Boneless breast/ turkey	1½ to 2 days	3 to 5 hours

THE BEST WAY TO ROAST TURKEY

At Butterball, we have tried every way of cooking turkey imaginable, and we keep coming back to what we consider the very best way to roast a whole bird or breast. You may have your own kitchen secrets, but once you try our open-pan roasting method, we are convinced you will find it the most satisfactory and trouble-free way to ensure perfectly cooked, moist, flavorful, golden turkey. On the other hand, there will be times when you want to grill or microwave the turkey. No problem. We have surefire ways for both with tasty results.

The Open-Pan Roasting Method: This cooking process is easy and appropriate for thawed and fresh turkey. There are 8 easy steps to follow—steps that will lead you from the kitchen to the dining table carrying a glorious, succulent, golden roast turkey.

1. Thaw the turkey in the refrigerator or in cold water (page 7). Remove the thawed or fresh turkey from its wrapper. Preheat the oven to 325°F.

2. Remove the neck from the body cavity and giblets from the neck cavity and refrigerate them. Drain the juices and blot the cavities with paper towels. Clean all work surfaces and utensils touched by raw turkey or juices with hot, soapy water. This, of course, includes your hands, cutting boards, counter tops, and knives.

3. Stuff the neck and body cavities, if desired and depending on the recipe. Turn the wings back to hold the neck skin in place. If the legs are untucked, return them to a tucked position. There is no need to truss the turkey.

4. Place the turkey, breast up, on a flat rack in an open roasting pan that is about 2 inches deep. Remember that a handy Turkey Lifter is packed with each Butterball turkey.

5. Insert a meat thermometer deep into the thickest part of the thigh next to the body. Be sure it does *not* touch the bone.

6. Brush the skin with vegetable oil to prevent it from drying out during roasting. Further basting is unnecessary.

7. Roast the turkey in the preheated 325°F. oven. When the skin turns golden brown, about two-thirds of the way through roasting, shield the breast loosely with lightweight foil to prevent overbrowning. For cooking times, see the chart below.

8. Check for doneness by looking at the meat thermometer. The internal temperature of the thigh should be 180 to 185°F. The temperature at the center of the stuffing should be 160 to 165°F. The thigh and drumstick meat should feel soft when pressed and when the thigh is pierced with a fork or skewer, the juices should run clear, not pink. When done, let the turkey stand for 15 to 20 minutes to make carving easy.

OPEN-PAN ROASTING METHOD TIME SCHEDULES

(Approximate cooking times for turkeys roasted at 325°F. on shallow racks in 2-inch-deep open pans)

Net Weight	Stuffed	Unstuffed
9 to 12 pounds	3½ to 4 hours	3 to 3½ hours
12 to 16 pounds	4 to 4½ hours	3½ to 4 hours
16 to 20 pounds	4½ to 5 hours	4 to 4½ hours
20 to 24 pounds	5 to 6 hours	4½ to 5 hours

Stuffing the Turkey: Most people like stuffed turkey, although there are those turkey lovers who prefer to cook the stuffing or dressing separately in a casserole. In either case, allow ½ to ¾ cup of stuffing per person. In or out of the bird, everyone loves stuffing.

When stuffing a 10-pound or smaller turkey, estimate that you will need ½ cup of stuffing for every pound. For birds weighing more than 10 pounds, figure on ¾ cup of stuffing for every pound. For example, for an 8-pound turkey, you need to prepare 4 cups of stuffing; for a 15-pound bird you need to prepare 11¼ cups of stuffing.

Most likely you will want to make a bread-based stuffing. Six slices of fresh bread yield about 5 cups of soft bread cubes. Six slices of slightly stale bread—bread allowed to dry overnight—make about 4½ cups firmer bread cubes. Beginning on page 191 we have so many enticing recipes for stuffings and dressings, you will want to try them all. There are others, too, included in some of the recipes for roasted turkeys and turkey breasts. Turn the pages slowly so you can savor each recipe.

Stuff the body and neck cavities of the turkey lightly, making sure it is not packed too tightly. Never stuff the turkey until just before roasting. This is not a "do-ahead" project—turkeys stuffed ahead of time can result in unwanted bacterial growth. If there is extra stuffing, spoon it into a buttered casserole with a lid and refrigerate it. When the turkey has only 45 to 60 minutes left in the oven, slide the uncovered casserole in next to it to heat through. Serve it alongside the main event.

If organization and time are concerns—and let's face it, they almost always are!—get a head start on the stuffing by preparing the ingredients, chopping those that require it, and measuring others. Keep the moist and dry ingredients separate until you are ready to combine them. When the stuffing is mixed, do not wait too long before stuffing the turkey.

THE BEST WAY TO GRILL TURKEY

It is possible you have never considered grilling a turkey or turkey parts on the outdoor grill, but once you have tried it, you may find yourself firing up the grill even on cold, blustery days. But try it first on a sunny, summer day as the charcoal fire needs tending and regular checking. Also, grilling in cold weather demands more of the chef simply because more charcoal briquettes are necessary to maintain the temperature of the fire than are needed in the warm weather, and so the grill must be watched more diligently. If you have a gas grill, you need not worry about any of this—you can grill turkey anytime and reward yourself with the tasty results. In any case, use a covered grill for cooking whole turkeys or turkey breasts. Turkey parts, depending on the recipe, may be grilled on an open brazier.

We suggest positioning charcoal grills with wheels so that the leg without the wheel is headed into the wind. Grills without wheels should be positioned so that the handles head into the wind. Clean the grill rack with a metal brush and cold water, if it needs it (this procedure should be followed *after* cooking every time the grill is used; this way the rack is ready when you are). Spray the grill rack with nonstick cooking spray to prevent the turkey from sticking.

If you are using charcoal and plan to cook a whole turkey or a turkey breast, prepare the grill for the Indirect Method. This means separating the coals in the bed of the grill to leave room for a metal or foil drip pan nestled between them. The turkey or breast sits over the pan and during cooking the juices drip into it. The drip pan should be larger than the turkey. For a 22-inch grill, put 25 to 30 briquettes on each long side of the pan.

Burn the coals for about 30 minutes until they are covered with gray ash. Set the sprayed rack on its brackets with the handles over the coals—this makes it easier to add more briquettes during cooking.

Brush the turkey with oil and put it on the rack directly over the drip pan. If the grill is large enough and the turkeys small enough, it is a good idea to cook two at once—you can never have too much leftover turkey—and when grilling, the cooking time for two birds is the same as for one. Cover the grill, leaving the vents open. To maintain a temperature of about 325°F., add 5 to 8 fresh briquettes to the hot coals every hour. A 12-pound unstuffed turkey will take about 3 hours to cook, at which time the breast temperature should be 170 to 175°F. and the thigh 180 to 185°F.

Follow the same method for grilling a breast with the bone or without it and for grilling a boneless whole turkey. A breast of turkey with the bone-in takes 1½ to 2½ hours and the final temperature should be 170°F. in the thickest part. A boneless breast or whole turkey takes 1 to 1¾ hours and the final temperature should be 170 to 175°F. in the center.

If barbecue sauce or a sweetened glaze is part of the recipe, brush it on the turkey during the last half hour of cooking. Brushing it on any earlier will not add any additional flavor and it may burn.

After the turkey is cooked, there may be a narrow rosy band of meat just under the skin. This is caused by the charcoal combustion reacting with the meat pigment. It is not a sign of undercooked meat.

As already mentioned, weather conditions contribute to the heat of the fire and, therefore, to cooking times. This is true even in warm weather when the wind and humidity can influence the way the fire maintains its temperature. It is a good idea to place an oven thermometer on the grill rack to monitor the temperature. If necessary, adjust the number of briquettes or the controls of a gas grill to maintain medium heat (325 to 350°F.).

THE BEST WAY TO COOK TURKEY IN THE MICROWAVE OVEN

Cooking turkey in the microwave takes less time than cooking it in a conventional oven, but requires more attention. At Butterball, we developed methods for cooking whole turkey, breast of turkey (bone-in), boneless whole turkey, and boneless turkey breast. These methods ensure even cooking, safe final temperatures, and—best of all—tender, juicy meat. Keep in mind that turkeys will not brown in the microwave oven, which is why we suggest making the Browning Sauce. If you decide not to use the Browning Sauce, the outside of the cooked turkey will appear pale, but the color does not in any way indicate raw or undercooked meat.

Keep in mind that all microwaves behave slightly differently, depending on the wattage of the oven, the size of the oven cavity, and the temperature of the food. It may be necessary to adjust the times slightly to accommodate your oven. Our times are based on 600- to 700-watt microwave ovens.

Whole Turkey: Thaw the turkey, if necessary, in the refrigerator or in cold water, following the directions on page 7. The thawed turkey should be about 40°F. Prepare the turkey for roasting, according to steps 2 and 3 for open-pan roasting method (page 9). If you stuff the turkey, cover the opening to the stuffed cavity with plastic wrap to hold the stuffing in place. Keep in mind that metal deflects microwaves and causes arc-ing (sparking), so be sure not to use metal skewers to close the cavities.

Place the thawed turkey, breast down, in a microwave-safe dish. If the turkey tips, brace it with a microwave-safe item. Brush the back of the turkey with one tablespoon of the Browning Sauce.

BROWNING SAUCE

¼ cup butter, melted
¼ teaspoon paprika
⅛ teaspoon Kitchen Bouquet

Blend the ingredients in a small bowl or glass measuring cup. Stir well.

Cook the turkey according to the following cooking schedule for microwave cooking. Use the time closest to the weight of the turkey. We have gauged the weight to equal the net weight minus the 8-ounce gravy packet. Microwave the turkey on High (100 percent) power for Time 1 (see chart). If the microwave oven does not have a turntable, rotate the turkey a quarter turn and continue microwaving it for Time 2. If the oven has a turntable, microwave it on High (100 percent) power for the total minutes for Times 1 and 2. Do not allow the turkey to stand between cooking times.

MICROWAVE COOKING SCHEDULE
FOR STUFFED OR UNSTUFFED TURKEY

(Approximate cooking times for 625- to 700-watt
microwave ovens)

Times	Weight			
	4 pounds	5 pounds	6 pounds	7 pounds
	Breast side down at High (100 percent) power			
1	8 minutes	10 minutes	12 minutes	14 minutes
2	8 minutes	10 minutes	12 minutes	14 minutes
	Breast side up at Medium (50 percent) power			
3	8 minutes	10 minutes	12 minutes	14 minutes
4	8 minutes	10 minutes	12 minutes	14 minutes
5	8 minutes	10 minutes	12 minutes	14 minutes
6	8 minutes	10 minutes	12 minutes	14 minutes
total cooking time	48 minutes	1 hour	1 hour, 12 minutes	1 hour, 24 minutes

Times	Weight			
	8 pounds	9 pounds	10 pounds	11 pounds
	Breast side down at High (100 percent) power			
1	16 minutes	18 minutes	20 minutes	22 minutes
2	16 minutes	18 minutes	20 minutes	22 minutes

MICROWAVE COOKING SCHEDULE
FOR STUFFED OR UNSTUFFED TURKEY

(Approximate cooking times for 625- to 700-watt microwave ovens)

Times	Weight			
	8 pounds	9 pounds	10 pounds	11 pounds
	Breast side up at Medium (50 percent) power			
3	16 minutes	18 minutes	20 minutes	22 minutes
4	16 minutes	18 minutes	20 minutes	22 minutes
5	16 minutes	18 minutes	20 minutes	22 minutes
6	16 minutes	18 minutes	20 minutes	22 minutes
total cooking time	1 hour, 36 minutes	1 hour, 48 minutes	2 hours	2 hours, 12 minutes

Times	Weight
	12 pounds
	Breast side down at High (100 percent) power
1	24 minutes
2	24 minutes
	Breast side up at Medium (50 percent) power
3	24 minutes
4	24 minutes
5	24 minutes
6	24 minutes
total cooking time	2 hours, 24 minutes

Discard the drippings and invert the turkey in the pan so that it is breast up. If the turkey is stuffed, remove the plastic wrap. Brush with another tablespoon or two of the Browning Sauce and, if necessary, brace the turkey to keep it level in the pan.

Microwave the turkey on Medium (50 percent) power for Times 3, 4, and 5. If your microwave oven is not equipped with a turntable, rotate the bird a quarter turn between each time period. Discard the drippings after each time period and brush with more Browning Sauce. If the microwave has a turntable, discard the drippings and brush with Browning Sauce at two or three regular intervals. If the turkey browns too much—which it might on the wing tips or legs—shield the browned areas with light-weight aluminum foil, shiny side out.

After Time 5, check for doneness. A meat thermometer inserted deep into the thickest part of the thigh but not touching the bone should register 180 to 185°F. The temperature at the thickest part of the breast, but not touching the bone, should be 170°F. The center of the stuffing should be 160 to 165°F. If all these temperatures have not been reached, cook for the number of minutes indicated in Time 6. Recheck the temperatures and cook for longer, if necessary.

Take the turkey from the microwave and tent it with foil. Let the turkey stand for 15 minutes to make carving easier.

Boneless Turkey and Boneless Breast of Turkey: Thaw the turkey, if necessary, in the refrigerator or in cold water, following the directions on page 7. The thawed turkey should be about 40°F. Remove the outer netting and wrapper and leave the string netting on the turkey. Place the thawed turkey on a microwave-safe rack in a microwave-safe dish. For the boneless turkey, position it so that the dark meat is up.

Microwave on Defrost (30 percent) power for 24 to 26 minutes per pound of net weight. Divide the total cooking time into four equal intervals and, if the microwave is not equipped with a turntable, rotate the turkey or turkey breast a quarter turn after each interval. Discard the drippings with each turn or, if you have a turntable, three or four times during cooking. After the second interval, or halfway through cooking, turn the turkey over.

When the turkey or turkey breast is done, a microwave meat thermometer inserted into the center of the roast should read 170°F. for boneless breast and 175°F. for boneless turkey. Wrap the cooked turkey in foil and let it stand for 15 minutes before removing the netting and slicing for serving.

Breast of Turkey (bone-in): Thaw the turkey, if necessary, in the refrigerator or in cold water, following the directions on page 7. The thawed turkey should be about 40°F. Remove the wrapper. Place the thawed turkey, skin side down, in a microwave-safe dish and brush the sides with Browning Sauce (page 15 for recipe).

Cook the turkey for 14 to 16 minutes per pound of net weight (the net weight is figured minus the 8-ounce gravy packet). Divide the total time into three equal intervals. Microwave on High (100 percent) power for the first interval. Discard the drippings and then lay the turkey on its side. Brush it with more Browning Sauce.

Microwave on Medium (50 percent) power for the second interval. Discard the drippings and lay the turkey on its other side. Brush with Browning Sauce. Continue to microwave on Medium (50 percent) power for the last cooking interval. At the end of this time, the microwave meat thermometer should read 170°F. when inserted into the thickest part of the breast without touching the bone. Continue cooking at Medium (50 percent) power, if necessary. Cover the turkey with foil and let it stand for 15 minutes to make carving easier.

2

QUESTIONS AND ANSWERS FROM THE BUTTERBALL TURKEY TALK-LINE

ome people roast their turkey. Some people grill their turkey. Some people smoke their turkey. And some people burn their turkey.

Because there are so many ways to prepare the favorite Thanksgiving bird and because there are so many ways to ruin it, Butterball offers a universal grandmother to oversee the thousands of holiday cooks every November and December—The Turkey Talk-Line.

The Talk-Line takes these fledgling cooks under its wing each holiday season, soothing those chefs who wonder if their turkey will collapse if it's not stuffed and reassuring others who fear their turkey may explode if they do.

To some holiday cooks, the Talk-Line serves as a Lost and Found. Calls frequently ring into "Turkey Central" about acrylic nails accidentally mixed into the stuffing and missing rubber gloves that suddenly appear four hours later in one of the turkey cavities. Imaginative chefs ask if it's possible to pop popcorn inside the turkey while roasting, or if the dishwasher is a suitable place for cooking the bird.

The patient turkey ambassadors who staff the Butterball Turkey Talk-Line take any question from the basic ("How do I turn on my oven?") to the puzzling ("What should I do if I set my oven on self-clean instead of bake?") and offer helpful, courteous guidance for delicious, golden-brown and food-safe holiday birds.

Yet, when we instituted our Turkey Talk-Line in 1981 we had no idea how popular it would become or how much we would learn from it. From the first of November until the day before Christmas Eve (including all day Thanksgiving Day), 44 specially trained home economists chat with more than 270,000 consumers on a toll-free line (1-800-323-4848), answering their questions about turkey preparation. No wonder some folks have dubbed the Turkey Talk-Line "the granddaddy of the hotlines." From these conversations we at Butterball discovered that the holiday turkey is usually cooked by the same member of the household year in and year out, and that the cook almost always is a woman. We learned that 66 percent of our customers prefer to stuff the turkey before roasting it. And, guess what? Close to 30,000 holiday cooks snap pictures of their Thanksgiving and Christmas turkeys before they are happily devoured.

That's what we have learned, but what do you learn? An overwhelming number of callers (more than 15,000 in recent years) ask about our favorite way to roast a whole turkey. The answer? The open-pan roasting method (page 9). Next come queries on food safety, thawing, storage, meat thermometer insertion, testing for doneness, stuffing, preparation of the oven, basting, and how much turkey to buy. Callers of all description dial our Turkey Talk-Line, from new brides to restaurateurs and grandmothers. Many are first-time turkey cooks, still others are trying something different and need encouragement, while other turkey cooks are concerned about recent press reports on safety. We love talking about our favorite subject with our favorite people, our customers. We log every query on a computer and the 51 listed here represent the top 14 categories of questions asked, beginning with the most popular ones.

ROASTING YOUR BUTTERBALL TURKEY

1. *Do you have a favorite way of cooking a turkey?*

Yes, the open-pan roasting method. This method is described on page 9 and also in pamphlets packaged with every Butterball turkey.

2. *Why do you say the open-pan roasting method is the best?*

The open-pan roasting method is the easiest way to cook a turkey. No special equipment is needed and the bird will be golden brown and beautiful, tender and juicy, with a roasted flavor, which most people prefer to a steamed flavor.

3. *What do you do to make a turkey have a nice, shiny brown look?*

Just brush it with any vegetable oil (such as corn or canola) before putting it in the oven. About two-thirds through the roasting time, shield the breast with a tent of foil.

4. *I have a 16-pound turkey. How long will it take to cook?*

Stuffed and roasted, uncovered, at 325°F., it will take approximately 4½ hours. Unstuffed it will take 4 hours. See the chart on page 10 for more information.

5. *I have been roasting turkeys for 35 years and they are always dry. What am I doing wrong?*

You are probably cooking the turkey too long or the oven is too hot. We suggest trying the open-pan roasting method.

6. *Is it possible to have a tender turkey that looks as pretty as those I see in your advertisements?*

Absolutely! Just follow the open-pan roasting method on page 9.

7. *This will be my first turkey and I am scared to death that I will ruin it. Can you help?*

Don't be nervous. It's really easy. Buy a Butterball turkey and follow the directions that come with it. Read Chapter 1 of this book, too, for more hints. Start by thawing the turkey as directed, and continue from that point.

8. *The directions say "roast breast up." How do I know which side is the breast?*

The back is flat and it lies flush on the roasting rack. The breast is rounded with generous amounts of white meat.

9. *What size pan do I need for roasting a turkey?*

We recommend an open pan with 2 to 2½-inch sides. A small turkey (Li'l Butterball) under 9 pounds will fit nicely into a 13-by-11-inch cake pan. For larger birds, your pan needs to be 15 to 17 inches long and 10 to 12 inches wide.

FOOD SAFETY

10. *I did not realize I was not supposed to leave the turkey on the counter to thaw. Will it be okay to use?*

Next time, thaw the turkey in the refrigerator so that it stays safe. Read pages 7 to 8 for specific thawing directions. In this case, if the turkey is still cold to the touch and smells okay, it should be fine. Be sure to cook it properly and use a meat thermometer to check for doneness.

11. *We forgot to put the turkey away after dinner and it has been sitting out all night. Can we still eat it?*

We do not recommend that you do. Hazardous bacterial growth may have developed at room temperature after that long a time.

12. *You hear so much about salmonella poisoning these days. How can I be sure my family will not get it?*

First, raw poultry should always be refrigerated. Second, it should be cooked properly to internal temperatures of 170°F. in the breast and 180°F. in the thigh. Also, wash all counters, utensils, and surfaces that come in contact with the raw turkey and its juices with hot, soapy water.

THAWING TURKEY

13. *How much time will it take to thaw a 16-pound turkey?*

Left in its original wrapper on a tray in the refrigerator, it will take about 3 days. Thawed breast down submerged in cold water, it will take about 9 hours. Change the water frequently. Never thaw turkey at room temperature. Increased bacterial growth and spoilage can result. For further information, read pages 7 to 8.

14. *What should I do if my turkey thaws too soon?*

Thawed turkey can be kept in the refrigerator for up to 4 days.

15. *We have thawed a turkey and now find we have to go out of town for a week or two. Do we have to throw out the turkey?*

No. If the turkey is still icy cold it can be refrozen and will be perfectly safe to use. The texture may be affected by refreezing, although it still will taste good. If possible, cook the turkey, carve it, and store it in the freezer up to 2 months.

STORING TURKEY

16. *We have a turkey that has been in the freezer since last year. Is it safe to eat?*

Yes. Turkey that has been kept frozen for a year should be safe to eat. For maximum flavor, we recommend storing a turkey no longer than 6 or 7 months. If the turkey is stored longer than a year, you may want to use it for casseroles and soups.

17. *How long can I store cooked turkey?*

Three days in the refrigerator; 2 months in the freezer.

USING A MEAT THERMOMETER

18. *When do I put the thermometer in the turkey?*

Unless it is an instant-read thermometer, insert it before the turkey goes in the oven.

19. *Where does the meat thermometer go?*

The tip of the meat thermometer should be inserted in the thickest part of the thigh, between the body and the thigh bone but not touching the bone. Turn the thermometer so you can read it while the turkey is in the oven.

STUFFING A TURKEY

20. *Is it okay to stuff a turkey?*

Yes. But do so just before putting the turkey in the preheated oven. Do not stuff the turkey a day or even a few hours before roasting. It is also a good idea to use a meat thermometer to determine that the stuffing has reached 160°F. before removing it from the oven.

21. *How much stuffing should I prepare?*

For a turkey weighing more than 10 pounds, you will

need ¾ cup of stuffing per pound of turkey; for smaller turkeys, figure on ½ cup stuffing per pound of turkey.

22. *Where should I put the stuffing?*

There are two places. One is the body cavity, from which the turkey neck must be removed, and the other is the neck cavity, where you will find the package of giblets. Remove it.

23. *Should I truss the turkey to keep the stuffing inside?*

No. We think it is attractive for the stuffing to show in the body cavity opening. If you do not want the stuffing surface to be crunchy, cover it with a small piece of foil during roasting. To keep the stuffing in the neck cavity, use a trick called "wings akimbo." Bend the wings to the back of the bird and use the wing tips to hold the neck skin in place. In this position, the wings also hold the bird steady while it roasts.

24. *I do not want to stuff the turkey but my husband likes stuffing. What can we do?*

Put the stuffing in a buttered casserole. If you want a crisp top, bake it uncovered. It will take about 45 to 60 minutes in a 325°F. oven.

25. *My wife and I argue about whether our turkey is done. How can we tell for sure?*

A meat thermometer inserted in the thickest part of the thigh should read 180 to 185°F. The breast meat should be up to 170°F. and the stuffing up to 160 to 165°F.

26. *We don't have a meat thermometer. How can we know if the turkey is done?*

The juices that flow when the thigh is pierced with a fork should run clear or yellow, not pink, and the thigh meat should feel soft when pinched.

27. *Our turkey is done and we are not planning to eat for another hour. What should we do?*

Remove the turkey from the oven, leaving the stuffing in it. Cover with foil and clean towels to hold in the heat.

28. *Our guests are delayed by three hours. The turkey is done now. What should we do?*

Leave the stuffing in. Remove the turkey from the oven and cool the oven down to 150 to 200°F. Cover the turkey with aluminum foil and keep it in the warm oven until the guests arrive. It will be less juicy than if it had been served on time.

PREPARING A TURKEY FOR ROASTING

29. *I am going to be cooking my first turkey this year. What steps will I have to go through to get it ready for the oven?*

Remove the neck and giblets from the body and neck cavities. You may need to untuck the legs to do this. Drain the juices and use a paper towel to blot excess moisture from the cavities. You can stuff the cavities if you like. Put the wings in the akimbo position (see #23, above) and retuck the legs. Place the turkey breast up on a flat rack on top of the Turkey Lifter in a shallow open pan. Brush the skin with oil. Insert the meat thermometer.

30. *What kind of a pan will I need?*

For the open-pan roasting method, use an open pan with sides 2 to 2½ inches high. For the covered pan method, use a dark enamel roaster. The roasting time is about 30 minutes less than for the open-pan roasting method. Shiny aluminum pans deflect heat and therefore the cooking time is increased by as much as an hour if you are using this sort of pan for the covered pan method.

31. *You say to place the turkey on a rack. Do you mean the oven rack?*

Yes and no. The pan the turkey is in goes on the oven rack, but the turkey itself should be on a small rack *in* the pan. This allows heat to circulate underneath the bird and keeps the turkey from sitting in its own juices.

32. *I see there is a string gadget in with the recipe folder that came with my Butterball. What is it for?*

We call that the "string lifter." It is a Butterball exclusive. Place it on the rack under the turkey and then bring the loops up around the turkey. Do this before putting the turkey in the oven. When you are ready to lift the cooked turkey from the pan, use the loops as handles. There is a diagram in the directions folder.

33. *Shouldn't I add some water to the pan so the meat will be juicy?*

No. That is not necessary. The turkey will be juicy if you roast it at the gentle heat of 325°F. and do not overcook it.

34. *My mother always used butter to baste the turkey. You say to use oil. Why?*

Butter and margarine contain milk solids, which scorch. Oil or shortening keeps the skin moist without scorching. The oil also helps give a golden color. It is not necessary to baste the turkey while roasting.

35. *You do not say to salt the turkey in the cooking directions. Did you forget?*

No. The flavor will not penetrate the skin or the rib cage, so all salting would do is add saltiness to the gravy.

36. *I cannot believe you say it is not necessary to baste turkey. How am I going to be sure the turkey will be moist?*

Pouring juices over the surface of a turkey during roasting will not make the meat juicy. The liquid does not penetrate the skin. It just runs off and ends up in the drippings. What is more, every time you open the oven door to baste the turkey, you cool the oven and may prolong the cooking time.

37. *Has something been added to the meat of Butterball turkeys?*

Yes and no. Frozen Butterball turkeys have been deep-basted in the breast area. Fresh turkeys are not basted.

38. *Why are there basting ingredients added to frozen Butterball turkeys?*

They are added deep in the breast area to enhance juiciness and flavor.

39. *What are the basting ingredients? I hope there is no cholesterol in them.*

No, there is no cholesterol. The basting ingredients are a vegetable oil mixture, similar to a high-quality margarine. And we add only a small amount, three percent of the total weight of the bird.

40. *My friend and I have an argument. Isn't there butter in Butterball turkeys?*

No, and there never has been. The name Butterball refers to the generous rounded shape of our turkeys.

41. *I am wondering whether to buy a fresh turkey or a frozen one. What would you suggest?*

There are points in favor of buying both kinds. The choice has to be yours. Some factors to consider are that a fresh Butterball has not been deep-basted. So it is all natural and the breast meat will be somewhat drier. Fresh turkeys may be a good idea for people on certain special diets. But because they are fresh, they should be purchased shortly before you plan to use them. Frozen turkeys, on the other hand, can be purchased even months in advance. Just plan on enough thawing time and keep it cold when thawing in cold water or the refrigerator. If you consider thawing an inconvenience, fresh turkey might be your preference. Frozen turkeys are deep-basted in the breast to enhance juiciness and flavor. All Butterball turkeys are delicious.

42. *I bought a fresh Butterball turkey and I notice that the wrapper says "minimally processed." What does that mean?*

It simply means that the turkey has been cleaned and chilled.

BUYING A TURKEY

43. *I will be cooking for 16 people on Thanksgiving Day. How much turkey should I buy?*

A general rule of thumb is 1½ pounds of turkey per person. This gives you generous servings and some leftovers. But this is a flexible guideline and you need to consider how many hearty and how many light eaters there are in the group. We suggest you buy the biggest Butterball you can find. They go up to 24 pounds. Or you can buy two 12-pound birds for the same yield. This way, you will surely have enough and there will also be plenty of leftovers.

44. *No one at our house likes dark meat. Is there an all-white meat turkey?*

No. Drumsticks and thighs, which every turkey has, are considered dark meat. But you might enjoy using a breast of turkey (bone-in). It is essentially a whole turkey with the wings, thighs, and drumsticks removed so that it is all white meat. The cavity can even be stuffed, if you like.

45. *My wife has to work and I will be cooking Thanksgiving dinner for the kids. What is the easiest way to do this?*

We suggest a Frozen Stuffed Butterball turkey. These birds are already stuffed and are cooked while still frozen. You do not have to worry about thawing or stuffing the turkey. Just put the turkey in the roasting pan, brush it with oil, and roast it for the appropriate time. See page 10 for more information.

46. *The store advertisements talk about hen and tom turkeys. What is the difference? Is one better than the other? Why doesn't it say on the Butterball wrapper whether I am buying a hen or a tom?*

Larger turkeys, generally over 16 pounds, are toms. Smaller ones are hens. In terms of flavor, tenderness, or percentage of white meat, it makes no difference which you buy. Purchase the size that is right for your family or party, and do not worry about whether it is a tom or a hen.

USING AN OVEN BAG

47. *All my friends are talking about cooking their turkeys in one of the new oven cooking bags. Is it okay to cook turkeys that way?*

Yes, although it is not our preferred method. It is a safe way and many people like it. When you use an oven cooking bag, the turkey will have more of a steamed flavor. Also, the skin may stick to the bag and split, so you get a less-than-picture-perfect result. The oven bags come with directions, which should be followed carefully. Turkeys cook more quickly in the bags, so use a meat thermometer to be sure the stuffing reaches a temperature of 160°F.

BREAST OF TURKEY (BONE-IN)

48. *There will be only three of us for dinner and I thought I would cook a turkey breast, as we all like white meat. How do I go about it?*

The directions are essentially the same as for a whole turkey. You can even stuff the cavity, if you like. Put the breast, skin side up, on a flat rack in an open pan. Preheat the oven to 325°F., brush the breast with oil, insert a meat thermometer into the thickest part, not touching the bone, and cook until the thermometer registers 170°F. Protect the skin with a tent of foil when it is attractively golden brown. Read pages 19 to 20 for more information.

USING FOIL WHEN TURKEY ROASTING

49. *Shouldn't I cover the turkey with foil before I put it in the oven?*

Foil deflects heat away from the bird and lengthens the roasting time, so we suggest roasting the turkey, uncovered, until the skin is a beautiful golden brown. At this point, about two-thirds through the roasting time, use a piece of foil about the size of a piece of notebook paper, folded down the middle, to shield the breast.

50. *I do not have a pan big enough for a turkey. Are the heavy-duty foil ones you see in the grocery stores okay to use?*

Yes. We suggest you select one with sides 2½ to 3 inches high. Support the pan with a cookie sheet with sides, or use double foil pans to make the pan and turkey easier to handle.

51. *My mother used to wrap the turkey completely in foil for roasting. Do people still do it that way?*

Some do, especially if they are in a hurry. When using the foil-wrapped method, increase the oven temperature to 450°F. and do not stuff the turkey. The turkey cooks quickly and the heat does not have time to cook the stuffing thoroughly. The turkey will be less than picture-perfect and the meat will not have a roasted flavor. It also may be dry.

CARVING DIRECTIONS

Let turkey stand 15 to 20 minutes before carving. Cut band of skin holding drumsticks.

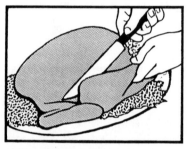

1. Grasp drumstick. Place knife beetween thigh and body of turkey and cut through skin to joint. Remove entire leg by pulling out and back, using point of knife to disjoint it. Separate thigh and drumstick at joint.

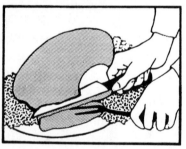

2. Insert fork in upper wing to steady turkey. With knife, make a long cut above wing joint through to body frame. Wing may be disjointed from body, if desired.

3. Slice straight down with an even stroke, beginning halfway up the breast. When knife reaches cut above wing bone, slice will fall free. Continue slicing white meat by starting cut at a higher point each time.

3

THE WHOLE TURKEY

I n this chapter we prepare turkey the old-fashioned way: We cook the entire bird. But if you think the following recipes will sound like those from Grandmother's recipe file, you have another think coming. These recipes are for lightly-herbed turkeys, turkeys stuffed with nothing more than fresh vegetables, and turkeys glazed with luscious fruit sauces. We rely on fresh and dried herbs and spices, tangy citrus fruit, and bold mustards. We even have a recipe for grilling a whole turkey on the backyard barbecue.

A number of recipes call for a big, magnificent turkey, the sort you are accustomed to seeing on the holiday table, but also included are numerous recipes for boneless whole turkeys and the small, family-sized birds we call Li'l Butterball.

OVEN-ROASTED
THANKSGIVING DINNER

Serves 8 to 10

This is a classic, and one that will make Thanksgiving dinner easier than ever since most of the vegetables are cooked alongside the turkey. The roasted vegetables take the place of stuffing, but if you can't live without it, make stuffing and follow the directions for cooking stuffed turkey on pages 10–11.

1 9- to 10-pound Butterball turkey or Li'l Butterball turkey, thawed if frozen
Vegetable oil
4 medium parsnips, peeled and cut diagonally into ½-inch slices
1 medium rutabaga, peeled and cut into ¾-inch chunks
2 large red potatoes, scrubbed and cut into ½-inch slices
8 ounces baby carrots, peeled and trimmed
1 large knob celery root, peeled and trimmed
1 bulb fennel, trimmed and cut crosswise into ¼-inch slices
10 medium shallots, peeled
8 tablespoons unsalted butter or margarine, melted
⅔ cup dry white vermouth or white grape juice
Coarse salt
Freshly ground black pepper

Preheat the oven to 325°F. Remove the neck and giblets from the turkey cavities. Refrigerate for another use.

Drain the turkey well. Turn the wings back to hold

the neck skin in place. Put the turkey, breast side up, on a flat rack in an open pan about 2 inches deep. Insert a meat thermometer into the thickest part of the thigh next to the body, being careful not to touch the bone. Brush the skin with vegetable oil to prevent drying. (Further basting is unnecessary.) Put the turkey in the oven. When the skin turns golden brown, cover the breast loosely with lightweight aluminum foil to prevent overbrowning.

Check the package or roasting directions on page 10 for roasting times. About 1½ hours before the turkey is done, put the vegetables in the roasting pan, surrounding the turkey. Drizzle the vegetables with the melted butter and vermouth and season with salt and pepper to taste. Roast the vegetables with the turkey, stirring occasionally.

Check the turkey for doneness: Internal thigh temperature should be 180 to 185°F. When the thigh is pierced, the juices should run clear, not pink.

Remove the turkey to a serving platter and let stand 15 to 20 minutes before carving. Keep the vegetables in a warm place and cover with aluminum foil until serving time. To serve, arrange the vegetables around the turkey on a platter.

ROAST TURKEY WITH DIJON MUSTARD SAUCE

Serves 10 to 12

We do something a little different here: We spread some mustard directly on the turkey meat under the skin. Loosening the skin for this application is a breeze and the cooked meat will be especially juicy and flavorful.

1 12- to 14-pound Butterball turkey, thawed if frozen
⅓ cup grainy Dijon mustard
Vegetable oil

Dijon Mustard Sauce

Turkey drippings
3 tablespoons all-purpose flour
1 cup half-and-half
¼ cup grainy Dijon mustard
¼ cup chopped parsley

Preheat the oven to 325°F. Remove the neck and giblets from the turkey cavities. Drain the turkey well. Free the legs from the tucked position, without cutting the band of skin. Using a rubber spatula or your hand, loosen the skin over the breast, starting at the body-cavity opening by the legs. Spread 2 tablespoons of mustard inside the body cavity and spread the remaining mustard on the meat under the skin. Hold the skin in place at the opening with toothpicks. Return the legs to the tucked position and turn the wings back to hold the neck skin in place.

Put the turkey, breast side up, on a flat rack in an open pan, about 2 inches deep. Insert a meat thermometer into the thickest part of the thigh next to the body, being careful not to touch the bone. Brush the turkey skin with vegetable oil.

Put the turkey in the oven and roast for 3½ to 3¾ hours. When the skin turns golden brown, cover the breast loosely with aluminum foil to prevent over-browning.

Check the turkey for doneness. The thigh temperature should be 180 to 185°F. Let the turkey stand for 15 to 20 minutes while you make the mustard sauce.

To make the mustard sauce, remove the fat from the turkey drippings with a turkey baster or skimming spoon and discard. Add enough water to the drippings to make 2 cups. In a medium saucepan, blend the drippings with the flour, using a wire whisk. Cook, stirring, over medium-high heat until the mixture thickens and starts to boil. Stir in the half-and-half, mustard, and parsley. Continue to cook over medium heat until the sauce is thickened but not boiling.

Carve the turkey and serve with the mustard sauce.

TURKEY WITH
LEMON-HERB DRESSING

Serves 6

In this straightforward recipe for roasting a fresh turkey, the fragrant dressing is cooked in a casserole rather than in the turkey's cavity. Lemon zest is the colored part of the lemon peel. Slice or peel it from the fruit carefully to avoid getting any of the bitter white pith.

1 7- to 8-pound fresh Li'l Butterball turkey

Dressing

2 tablespoons unsalted butter or margarine
¾ cup chopped celery
½ cup chopped onion
¼ cup chopped parsley
1½ teaspoons grated lemon zest
½ teaspoon dried marjoram
¼ teaspoon dried thyme
4 cups unseasoned dried bread cubes
1 cup chicken broth

Preheat the oven to 325°F. Roast the turkey according to package directions or by following the directions on pages 8–11.

About one hour before the turkey is done, make the dressing. Heat the butter in a medium saucepan over medium heat until melted. Add the celery and onion and cook until crisp-tender. Stir in the parsley, lemon zest, marjoram, and thyme. Put the bread cubes in a large bowl. Add the vegetable mixture and the broth, and toss to mix. Put the dressing in a buttered 1½-quart casserole and bake in the oven with the turkey for 45 minutes, or until hot.

Let the turkey stand for 15 to 20 minutes before carving. Serve the turkey with the dressing.

TURKEY WITH SAUSAGE AND ORANGE CORNBREAD STUFFING

Serves 10 to 12

We start with homemade cornbread lightly scented with orange and then make a classic sausage stuffing, using the cornbread in place of bread cubes. The stuffed turkey is delicious, or you may choose to cook the stuffing separately. Read the directions for cooking stuffed or unstuffed turkey on pages 8–11 before beginning. And try the cornbread by itself as a delightful side dish with cold sliced turkey or grilled turkey parts.

Orange Cornbread

1½ cups yellow cornmeal
½ cup all-purpose flour
2 tablespoons sugar
4 teaspoons baking powder
½ teaspoon salt
1 cup milk
1 large egg, beaten
⅓ cup vegetable oil
2 teaspoons finely shredded orange zest

Stuffing

½ roll (8 ounces) Eckrich Country Sausage
1 cup chopped onion

½ cup chopped green bell pepper
½ cup chopped celery
2 large eggs, beaten
1 teaspoon dried thyme, crushed
½ teaspoon salt
1 to 1¼ cups turkey or chicken broth

1 12- to 14-pound Butterball turkey, thawed if frozen

Preheat the oven to 400°F. Butter a 9 × 9 × 2-inch baking pan. To make the cornbread, combine the cornmeal, flour, sugar, baking powder, and salt in a medium bowl. Add the milk, egg, oil, and orange zest and stir just until combined (do not overmix). Pour the batter into the prepared pan and bake for 20 to 25 minutes. Remove the cornbread from the oven and let cool completely. Lower the oven temperature to 325°F.

Crumble the cooled cornbread and set aside.

To make the stuffing, put the sausage in a large skillet over medium heat, using a wooden spoon to break up the meat. Add the onion, green pepper, and celery and cook until the sausage is browned and the vegetables are tender. Drain off the fat.

In a large bowl, combine the sausage mixture with the eggs, thyme, and salt. Add the crumbled cornbread and toss to mix. Add enough broth to moisten, and toss.

Prepare the turkey for roasting, lightly stuffing the neck and body cavities. Roast the stuffed turkey according to package directions or by following the directions on pages 8–11. Alternatively, roast the turkey unstuffed and bake the stuffing separately: Put the stuffing in a buttered 2½-quart casserole, cover, and bake with the turkey for 1 hour or until hot.

Let the turkey stand for 15 to 20 minutes before carving.

TURKEY WITH GARLIC AND CHILI PEPPER STUFFING

Serves 12 to 14

The Tex-Mex stuffing for this turkey is heady with the flavor of garlic and mild green chili peppers. Green chili peppers are sold in cans in the aisle of the supermarket devoted to Mexican food.

Stuffing

⅓ cup unsalted butter or margarine
2 medium red bell peppers, seeded and chopped
½ cup chopped onion
4 to 5 large cloves garlic, minced
2 4-ounce cans diced green chili peppers, drained
¼ cup chopped parsley
¼ teaspoon salt
¼ teaspoon ground red pepper
8 cups dried whole-wheat or white bread cubes
1½ cups (6 ounces) shredded cheddar cheese
¾ to 1 cup chicken broth

1 14- to 16-pound Butterball turkey, thawed if frozen

Preheat the oven to 325°F.

To make the stuffing, heat the butter in a medium saucepan over medium heat. Add the bell peppers, onion, and garlic and cook until crisp-tender. Stir in the chili peppers, parsley, salt, and red pepper.

In a large bowl, combine the vegetable mixture with the bread cubes and cheese. Add enough broth to moisten and toss to combine.

Prepare the turkey for roasting, lightly stuffing the neck and body cavities. Roast the stuffed turkey according to package directions or by following the directions on pages 8–11. Alternatively, roast the turkey unstuffed and bake the stuffing separately: Put the stuffing in a buttered 2½-quart casserole, cover, and bake with the turkey for 1 hour or until hot.

Let the turkey stand for 15 to 20 minutes before carving.

TURKEY WITH
APPLE-RAISIN HERB STUFFING

Serves 10 to 12

Because they are readily available and firm and tart, we suggest using bright green Granny Smith apples, but you may substitute any firm, crisp, tart apple. Golden raisins are also known as sultanas. They are easy to find but if you cannot, use dark raisins instead.

Stuffing

8 cups slightly dried white or whole-wheat bread cubes (10 to 12 slices bread, cubed and dried overnight)
3 cups coarsely chopped Granny Smith apples (3 medium apples)
¾ cup golden raisins
⅓ cup chopped onion
⅓ cup chopped parsley
1½ teaspoons rubbed sage
1 teaspoon dried thyme
1 teaspoon dried rosemary, crushed
1 cup chicken broth
6 tablespoons unsalted butter or margarine, melted

1 12- to 14-pound Butterball turkey, thawed if frozen

Preheat the oven to 325°F.

To make the stuffing, combine the bread cubes, apples, raisins, onion, parsley, and dried herbs in a large bowl. Add the broth and melted butter and toss to mix.

Prepare the turkey for roasting, lightly stuffing the neck and body cavities. Roast the stuffed turkey according to package directions or by following the directions on pages 8–11. Alternatively, roast the turkey unstuffed and bake the stuffing separately: Put the stuffing in a buttered 2½-quart casserole, cover, and bake with the turkey for 1 hour or until hot.

Let the turkey stand for 15 to 20 minutes before carving.

TURKEY WITH CRANBERRY-SAUSAGE STUFFING

Serves 10 to 12

Sausage adds flavor and moisture to stuffing, and its rich flavor blends well with the milder flavor of roast turkey. Fresh cranberries add a tart fruity taste. Cranberries should be cut in half before they are added to the stuffing mixture, but if the task seems too daunting, chop them very briefly *in the food processor or blender. Be careful not to pulverize them. When buying fresh cranberries, it is a good idea to purchase several bags at a time as they freeze beautifully and are available in the markets for such a short time. This way you can enjoy them any time of year.*

Stuffing

1 8-ounce package Brown 'N Serve sausage links, original variety
4 tablespoons unsalted butter or margarine
1 cup chopped celery
1 cup chopped onion
1 16-ounce package herb-seasoned stuffing cubes
1 cup fresh cranberries, cut in half
2 teaspoons rubbed sage
2 cups chicken broth

1 12- to 14-pound Butterball turkey, thawed if frozen

Preheat the oven to 325°F.

To make the stuffing, cut the sausage links into pieces. Heat the butter in a medium saucepan over medium heat. Add the sausage, celery, and onion and cook until the vegetables are crisp-tender.

In a large bowl, combine the stuffing mix with the sausage mixture, cranberries, and sage. Add the broth and stir to mix.

Prepare the turkey for roasting, lightly stuffing the neck and body cavities. Roast the stuffed turkey according to package directions or by following the directions on pages 8–11. Alternatively, roast the turkey unstuffed and bake the stuffing separately: Put the stuffing in a buttered 2½-quart casserole, cover, and bake with the turkey for 1 hour or until hot.

Let the turkey stand for 15 to 20 minutes before carving.

TURKEY WITH ONION BREAD STUFFING

Serves 12

The stuffing for this whole turkey is made from plain bread cubes seasoned with onion, garlic, savory, nutmeg, and a good measure of grated cheese.

Stuffing

8 tablespoons (1 stick) unsalted butter or margarine
2 large onions, halved and sliced
2 cloves garlic, minced
½ teaspoon ground savory
¼ teaspoon grated nutmeg
1 12-ounce package unseasoned toasted white or
    whole-wheat bread cubes
¾ cup grated Parmesan cheese
½ cup sliced scallions (¼-inch slices)
1½ cups chicken broth

1 14-pound Butterball turkey, thawed if frozen
Vegetable oil

Preheat the oven to 325°F.

Heat the butter in a large skillet over medium heat. Add the onions and cook, stirring, for 6 to 7 minutes until softened. Stir in the garlic, savory, and nutmeg.

Combine the stuffing cubes, cheese, and scallions in a large bowl. Add the onion mixture and the broth and toss together.

Prepare the turkey for roasting, lightly stuffing the neck and body cavities. Brush the turkey with vegetable oil and roast according to package directions or follow the directions on pages 8–11. Alternatively, roast the turkey unstuffed and bake the stuffing separately: Put the stuffing in a buttered 2½-quart casserole, cover, and bake with the turkey for 1 hour or until hot.

Let the turkey stand for 15 to 20 minutes before carving.

TURKEY WITH TART CHERRY STUFFING

Serves 10

Once you discover the goodness of tart cherries used in savory preparations you will be as enthusiastic about them as we are. Try them in this fruit-filled stuffing for a special treat.

Stuffing

2 tablespoons unsalted butter or margarine
¾ cup chopped celery
⅓ cup chopped onion
¾ teaspoon dried thyme
¼ teaspoon poultry seasoning
1 7-ounce package herb-seasoned stuffing cubes
¾ cup golden raisins
¾ cup chicken broth
1 16-ounce can tart red cherries, drained

1 12-pound Butterball turkey, thawed if frozen
Vegetable oil

Preheat the oven to 325°F.

Heat the butter in a medium saucepan over medium heat. Add the celery and onion and cook, stirring, for about 5 minutes or until crisp-tender. Stir in the thyme and poultry seasoning.

In a large bowl, toss together the stuffing cubes, raisins, and celery mixture. Stir in the broth. Add the cherries and gently stir to mix.

Prepare the turkey for roasting, lightly stuffing the neck and body cavities. Brush the turkey with vegetable oil and roast according to package directions or follow the directions on pages 8–11. Alternatively, roast the turkey unstuffed and bake the stuffing separately: Put the stuffing in a buttered 2½-quart casserole, cover, and bake with the turkey for 1 hour or until hot.

Let the turkey stand for 15 to 20 minutes before carving.

ROAST TURKEY WITH CANADIAN BACON GRAVY

Serves 10 to 12

Chopped Canadian bacon is added to the robust gravy, giving it a smoky flavor and great texture. Canadian bacon is thicker, leaner, and less salty tasting than other bacon. You can buy it in many supermarkets and butcher shops.

---

3 medium carrots, cut into 2-inch pieces
2 stalks celery, cut into 2-inch pieces
1 medium onion, cut into eighths
2 large cloves garlic, cut into halves
½ cup parsley sprigs
1 large bay leaf
1 12- to 14-pound Butterball turkey, thawed if frozen
Vegetable oil
Turkey or chicken broth
6 tablespoons all-purpose flour
2 teaspoons grainy Dijon mustard
½ cup finely chopped Canadian bacon
2 tablespoons thinly sliced scallions

Preheat the oven to 325°F.

Combine the carrots, celery, onion, garlic, parsley, and bay leaf in a large bowl. Prepare the turkey for roasting. Stuff the body cavity with the vegetable mixture. Brush the turkey with vegetable oil and roast according to package directions or follow the directions on pages 8–11.

When the turkey is done, remove from the oven and let stand for 15 to 20 minutes before carving. Discard the vegetables.

Meanwhile, make the gravy. Pour the turkey drippings from the roasting pan into a 4-cup measure. Remove ¼ cup of fat from the drippings using a turkey baster or skimming spoon and put the fat into a saucepan. Skim off the remaining fat from the drippings and discard. Add enough turkey or chicken broth to the remaining drippings to make 3 cups. Add the flour to the fat in the saucepan and stir until blended. Gradually stir in the drippings and mustard and cook, stirring, over medium heat until the gravy comes to a boil and thickens, about 5 minutes. Stir in the Canadian bacon and the scallions.

ROAST TURKEY WITH HERB GRAVY

Serves 10 to 12

Leeks impart gentle, oniony flavor to stuffings and other savory preparations. For some reason they have acquired a reputation as a "fancy" ingredient, when in fact they are easy to grow and exceptionally hardy; in France they are considered everyday fare. Leeks are most available in the late summer and well into the fall, although they are found with increasing frequency all year round. Wash them well before using as they tend to be gritty and sandy. Trim the root end, make a shallow crosslike slash in the base, and soak in a sinkful of cold water for 10 to 15 minutes to rid them of sand. Rinse and drain well before cooking.

2 small tart apples, cored and cut into eighths
2 leeks, quartered lengthwise and cut into 2-inch pieces
⅓ cup coarsely chopped fresh sage, optional
2 bay leaves
1 tablespoon rubbed sage
1 tablespoon dried thyme
1 12- to 14-pound Butterball turkey, thawed if frozen
Vegetable oil
⅓ cup all-purpose flour
2 teaspoons chicken bouillon granules
Dash of freshly ground black pepper

Preheat the oven to 325°F.

Combine the apples, leeks, and herbs in a large bowl. Prepare the turkey for roasting. Stuff the neck and body cavities with the apple-herb mixture. Brush the turkey with vegetable oil and roast according to package directions or by following the directions on pages 8–11.

Remove the turkey from the oven and let stand 15 to 20 minutes before carving. Discard the apples and leeks.

Meanwhile, make the gravy. Pour the turkey drippings from the roasting pan into a 4-cup measure. Remove ¼ cup fat from the drippings using a turkey baster or skimming spoon and put the fat into a saucepan. Skim off and discard the remaining fat from the drippings. Add water to the drippings to make 3 cups. Blend the flour into the fat and stir until smooth. Gradually stir in the drippings, chicken bouillon granules, and pepper. Cook over medium heat, stirring, until the gravy thickens and boils, about 5 minutes.

ROAST TURKEY WITH LEMON-BASIL GRAVY

Serves 10 to 12

The lively combination of lemons and basil makes this gravy extra good. Only attempt making it, though, when you can find fresh basil; this basic roast will not taste the same without it.

3 carrots, cut into 2-inch pieces
2 stalks celery, cut into 2-inch pieces
1 large onion, cut into eighths
1 lemon, cut into 6 pieces
4 large cloves garlic, cut in half
1 cup coarsely chopped or torn fresh basil
½ cup parsley sprigs
1 12- to 14-pound Butterball turkey, thawed if frozen
Vegetable oil
¼ cup cornstarch
1 teaspoon chicken bouillon granules
½ teaspoon salt
Dash of freshly ground black pepper

Preheat the oven to 325°F.

Combine the vegetables, lemon, garlic, and herbs in a large bowl. Prepare the turkey for roasting. Stuff the neck and body cavities with the lemon-basil mixture. Brush the turkey with vegetable oil and roast according to package directions or follow the directions on pages 8–11.

Remove the turkey from the oven and let stand 15 to 20 minutes before carving. Discard the vegetables and lemon.

Meanwhile, make the gravy. Pour the turkey drippings from the roasting pan into a 4-cup measure. Remove 3 tablespoons fat from the drippings with a turkey baster or skimming spoon and put in a saucepan. Skim off and discard the remaining fat from the drippings. Add water to the drippings to make 3 cups. Blend the cornstarch into the fat and stir until smooth. Gradually stir in the drippings, chicken bouillon granules, salt, and pepper. Cook over medium heat, stirring, until the gravy thickens and boils, about 5 minutes.

APRICOT-MUSTARD GLAZED TURKEY

Serves 6

In this recipe a whole turkey is grilled over charcoal or on a gas-fired grill. The tangy, fruity glaze is perfect for warm-weather dining.

---

1 7-pound Li'l Butterball turkey, thawed if frozen
Vegetable oil
1 cup apricot preserves
¼ cup grainy Dijon mustard
⅛ teaspoon salt
Dash of ground cinnamon

Prepare a charcoal or gas grill for the indirect method of grilling by following the directions on pages 12–14.

Brush the turkey with vegetable oil and put on the cooking rack over a drip pan. Cover the grill and cook according to package directions or the directions on pages 8–11.

Meanwhile, prepare the apricot-mustard sauce. In a small bowl, stir together the preserves, mustard, salt, and cinnamon, breaking up any large pieces of apricot. Reserve ⅓ cup for the glaze. To glaze the turkey, brush several times with the reserved ⅓ cup sauce during the last 30 minutes of cooking time.

When the turkey is done, let it stand for 15 minutes. Slice the turkey and serve with the remaining apricot-mustard sauce.

TURKEY CREOLE

Serves 8

Cooking a whole boneless turkey is a good way to serve a lot of people without having to allow for the time it takes to roast a whole turkey still on its frame. This one is a little spicy, and so we suggest offsetting its "fire" with cooked rice.

---

1 3-pound Butterball boneless turkey, thawed if frozen
Vegetable oil
½ teaspoon salt
¼ teaspoon freshly ground black pepper
¼ teaspoon ground red pepper
¼ teaspoon paprika
¼ teaspoon chili powder
¼ teaspoon ground allspice
6 cups cooked rice

Preheat the oven to 325°F.

Brush the turkey with vegetable oil. Combine the seasonings and sprinkle them over the turkey. Roast the turkey according to package directions or by following the directions on pages 8–11.

When the turkey is done, remove it from the oven, wrap it in aluminum foil, and let stand for 10 to 15 minutes. Remove the netting from the turkey and slice. Serve with rice.

TURKEY WITH
SWEET POTATOES AND PEARS

Serves 8

The fruity sauce for this turkey is made with the juice from the sweet potato–pear casserole and the flavorful turkey drippings.

---

1 3-pound Butterball boneless turkey, thawed if frozen
3 medium sweet potatoes, peeled and cut into eighths
3 firm green pears, cored and cut into eighths
1 cup orange juice
1 tablespoon sugar
2 teaspoons spicy brown mustard
Dash of ground cinnamon
½ cup seedless green or red grapes, cut in half

Preheat the oven to 325°F. Roast the turkey according to the package directions or follow the directions on pages 8–11.

Meanwhile, put the sweet potatoes and pears in a shallow 2-quart casserole. Combine the orange juice, sugar, mustard, and cinnamon in a small bowl. Pour the mixture over the potatoes and pears. Cover the casserole and bake with the turkey for 1¼ hours.

When the turkey is done, remove it from the oven. Wrap it in aluminum foil and let it stand for 10 to 15 minutes. Meanwhile, in a small saucepan, combine the drippings with the orange juice mixture from the casserole, add the grapes, and bring to a boil. Simmer for 3 minutes.

Remove the netting from the turkey, slice the turkey, and serve with the sweet potatoes and pears and the sauce.

TURKEY WITH SAUERKRAUT AND APPLES

Serves 8

If your family prefers white meat only, try this quick and easy autumn meal with boneless turkey breast instead. Sauerkraut deserves more recognition than an occasional appearance on top of a hot dog. Gently sweetened with brown sugar, combined with crisp, fall apples, and heated through, sauerkraut takes on a subtleness rarely associated with it. Use your favorite apples in the recipe, remembering that those with red skin will look the prettiest in the dish.

---

1 3-pound Butterball boneless turkey, thawed if frozen
Vegetable oil
½ teaspoon salt
½ teaspoon freshly ground black pepper
½ teaspoon dry mustard
¼ teaspoon caraway seed
1 32-ounce jar sauerkraut, drained
3 tablespoons light brown sugar
2 medium tart apples, cut into wedges

Preheat the oven to 325°F.

Brush the turkey with vegetable oil. Combine the salt, pepper, mustard, and caraway seed and sprinkle evenly over the turkey. Roast the turkey according to package directions or follow the directions on pages 8–11.

Combine the sauerkraut with the sugar. About 30 minutes before the end of the roasting time, spoon the sauerkraut around the turkey, and top it with the apples.

Remove the cooked turkey from the pan. Wrap in aluminum foil and let stand 10 to 15 minutes. Keep the sauerkraut and apples warm. Remove the netting from the turkey. Slice the turkey and serve with the sauerkraut and apples.

4

TURKEY BREAST

More people prefer white meat to dark, so our all-white-meat breast is ideal. White meat is lower in calories and fat, too, which adds to its popularity. And turkey breasts are generally smaller than a whole bird and, therefore, more practical for today's family.

Turkey breasts can be purchased on the frame or boneless. They can be stuffed or not, glazed, basted, or grilled. The mild-tasting meat is a superb match with flavorful sauces and compotes—and no one argues with the leftovers!

GINGER PEACH–GLAZED
TURKEY BREAST

Serves 8

Mild-flavored turkey breast is a perfect match for this gingery fruit glaze and sauce. Teriyaki sauce is available in the Chinese or Oriental food section of the supermarket and in Asian markets.

1 8-pound Butterball breast of turkey, thawed if frozen
1 12-ounce jar peach preserves
1 tablespoon fresh lemon juice
1½ teaspoons teriyaki sauce
1 teaspoon ground ginger

Preheat the oven to 325°F. Roast the turkey according to package directions or follow the directions on pages 8–11.

Meanwhile, make the ginger peach sauce. Combine the preserves, lemon juice, teriyaki sauce, and ginger in a small saucepan and heat over medium heat, stirring until heated through. About 30 minutes before the turkey is done, brush with some of the sauce.

Let the turkey stand for 10 to 15 minutes before carving. Serve with the remaining sauce, warmed.

CRANBERRY-GLAZED
TURKEY BREAST

Serves 8

This recipe is similar to the preceding one for ginger peach–glazed breast of turkey, but here the flavors are reminiscent of a warm New England farmhouse kitchen rather than the Orient.

1 8-pound Butterball breast of turkey, thawed if frozen
1 14-ounce jar cranberry-orange sauce
¼ cup orange-flavored liqueur
½ teaspoon ground ginger
½ teaspoon ground cinnamon

Preheat the oven to 325°F. Roast the turkey according to package directions or follow the directions on pages 8–11.

Meanwhile, make the cranberry sauce. In a saucepan combine the cranberry-orange sauce, liqueur, ginger, and cinnamon and heat until warm. About 30 minutes before the turkey is done, brush with some of the sauce.

Let the turkey stand for 10 to 15 minutes before carving. Serve with the remaining warm sauce.

HERBED TURKEY

Serves 8

A turkey breast roasted with aromatic herbs is great for dinner and almost better as leftovers. Make sure you keep your herb pantry up to date by replacing the jars every three or four months. Store dried herbs in a cool, dark cupboard—not on a rack over the stove where heat and light contribute to their deterioration and loss of flavor.

---

1 8-pound Butterball breast of turkey, thawed if frozen
Vegetable oil
1 teaspoon parsley flakes
¼ teaspoon onion powder
¼ teaspoon garlic powder
½ teaspoon rubbed sage
½ teaspoon oregano leaves
¼ teaspoon salt
¼ teaspoon freshly ground black pepper

Preheat the oven to 325°F. Brush the turkey with vegetable oil. Combine the remaining ingredients and sprinkle the mixture over the turkey.

Roast the turkey according to package directions or follow the directions on pages 8–11.

Let the turkey stand for 10 to 15 minutes before carving.

APPLE-GLAZED
TURKEY BREAST ROAST

Serves 4 to 6

Serving a turkey breast half is a smart way to feed a small family or gathering, particularly if you do not want left-overs the next day. The small pieces of breast meat cook in less time than whole breasts and, like all Butterball turkeys, are succulent and delicious.

1 1½-pound Butterball fresh boneless turkey breast
    roast
Vegetable oil
½ cup apple jelly
1 teaspoon prepared mustard
½ teaspoon dried marjoram leaves

Preheat the oven to 325°F.

Put the breast roast, skin side up, on a rack in a shallow open pan. Brush the skin with vegetable oil. Bake for 1 to 1¼ hours or until a meat thermometer inserted in the thickest portion reads 170°F.

To make the glaze, combine the jelly, mustard, and marjoram in a small saucepan. Cook over low heat until the jelly is melted. Spoon 2 tablespoons of the glaze over the turkey about 15 minutes before the end of the cooking time.

Let the turkey stand 10 minutes before slicing. Pass the remaining glaze separately.

PECAN-STUFFED TURKEY BREAST WITH ASPARAGUS

Serves 4

Boneless Slice 'N Serve turkey breast is already cooked, so all you have to do is heat it through. In this recipe, cut about one pound of the breast into four equal slices, each one thick enough to cut a pocket in its side. Use a sharp knife to slit the meat, making a cut about 2½ inches long and 2½ inches deep.

1-pound piece of Butterball Slice 'N Serve breast of turkey
½ cup water
3 tablespoons unsalted butter or margarine, divided
1 cup crumbled dry stuffing mix
4 tablespoons chopped pecans, divided
1 teaspoon onion powder
½ teaspoon paprika
1 cup sliced mushrooms
1 cup fresh asparagus pieces
1 tablespoon cornstarch
1 cup half-and-half
1 large egg yolk, beaten
½ cup sliced scallions
1 tablespoon dry sherry
½ teaspoon salt

Preheat the oven to 350°F. Cut the turkey into 4 thick slices, about ¾-inch thick. Cut a pocket in the side of each slice.

Put the water and 1 tablespoon of the butter in a small saucepan. Bring to a boil over medium heat. Stir in the stuffing mix and 2 tablespoons of the pecans. Fill the pockets with the stuffing, packing it firmly but not tightly. Sprinkle the turkey slices with onion powder and paprika. Put the stuffed slices in an 8 × 8 × 2-inch baking dish.

Melt the remaining 2 tablespoons butter in a large saucepan over medium heat. Add the mushrooms and asparagus pieces and cook, stirring, for about 4 minutes or until the asparagus are crisp-tender. Combine the cornstarch and half-and-half and stir until smooth. Add the mixture to the vegetables and cook until thickened. Gradually stir ½ cup of the half-and-half mixture into the egg yolk. Add the yolk mixture to the pan and cook until bubbling. Stir in the scallions, sherry, salt, and the remaining 2 tablespoons pecans.

Spoon the asparagus mixture over the stuffed turkey slices and bake for 20 to 25 minutes or until hot.

GRILLED TURKEY BREAST WITH PINEAPPLE RELISH

Serves 4 to 6

In this recipe the meat of the turkey is seasoned with grated fresh ginger and freshly ground black pepper prior to cooking. To do that, lift the skin partially off the turkey, add the seasonings, then smooth the skin back over the meat, securing it with toothpicks. Use a sharp knife to help loosen the skin. The skin holds in the flavor of the spices as the turkey grills or oven-roasts.

Pineapple Relish

1 8-ounce can unsweetened crushed pineapple, undrained
¼ cup finely chopped celery
2 tablespoons finely chopped red onion
1 tablespoon finely chopped parsley
1 tablespoon fresh lime juice
½ teaspoon grated fresh ginger
Dash of salt

1 1½-pound Butterball fresh boneless turkey breast roast
½ teaspoon grated fresh ginger
Dash of freshly ground black pepper
Vegetable oil

To make the relish, combine the first 7 ingredients in a small bowl and let stand at cool room temperature for 1 to 2 hours to let the flavors blend.

Prepare a charcoal or gas grill for the indirect grilling method by following the directions on pages 12–14. Or preheat the oven to 325°F.

Loosen the skin along one edge of the turkey breast and carefully fold the skin back to expose the meat. Spread the ginger and pepper on the meat. Bring the skin back over the breast and secure with toothpicks. Brush with vegetable oil.

Grill the turkey breast over medium heat or roast in an 8 × 8 × 2-inch baking dish in the oven for 1 to 1¼ hours or until a meat thermometer inserted in the thickest part of the roast registers 170°F.

Cover the turkey breast with aluminum foil and let stand 10 minutes before slicing. Serve with the pineapple relish.

TURKEY WITH
APPLE-PEAR DRESSING

Serves 8

The bread for this dressing is raisin bread, so that you get the sweetness of raisins as well as the freshness of apples and pears. Serve with the Apple-Cinnamon Sauce on page 258.

1 8-pound Butterball breast of turkey, thawed if frozen
3 tablespoons unsalted butter or margarine
1 cup unpeeled chopped red apple
1 cup unpeeled chopped firm pear
½ cup large pecan pieces
¼ cup maple syrup
8 cups raisin bread cubes (10 to 12 slices bread)
½ cup chicken broth or water

Roast the turkey breast according to the package directions or follow the directions on pages 8–11. Alternatively, grill the turkey breast, using the indirect method described on pages 12–14.

While the turkey is roasting, prepare the dressing. Melt the butter in a large skillet over medium heat. Add the apple and pear and cook for about 4 minutes. Add the pecans and maple syrup and cook for 1 minute more.

Put the bread cubes in a large bowl. Add the fruit mixture and stir to combine. Stir in the broth. Return the dressing to the skillet, cover, and cook over low heat for 10 to 12 minutes, stirring occasionally. Alternatively, put the dressing in a buttered 2-quart casserole, cover, and bake with the turkey for the last 30 minutes of roasting time.

Let the turkey stand for about 10 minutes before carving. Serve with the dressing.

GRILLED TURKEY BREAST WITH TOMATO-JICAMA SALSA

Serves 8

An integral part of the Southwestern-inspired salsa used here is jícama. Pronounced HEEK-a-ma, the root vegetable is common in Mexican and other Central American cooking and has a flavor and texture similar to a water chestnut. The knobby vegetable is easy to find in most markets throughout the southern regions of the country and is turning up with frequency in other parts of North America, too.

1 8-pound Butterball breast of turkey, thawed if frozen
Vegetable oil

Tomato-Jícama Salsa

2 cups seeded and chopped tomato
1 cup peeled and diced *jícama*
½ cup chopped celery
¼ cup finely chopped red onion
1½ tablespoons chopped fresh cilantro
¼ cup red wine vinegar
2 tablespoons vegetable oil
2 tablespoons fresh lime juice
½ teaspoon ground cumin
¼ teaspoon salt

Prepare a gas or charcoal grill for the indirect method of grilling by following the directions on pages 12–14. Brush the turkey lightly with vegetable oil and set it, skin side up, on the grill rack over a drip pan. Cover the grill and cook for 2 to 2½ hours, until a meat thermometer inserted into the thickest part of the breast registers 170°F.

Meanwhile, prepare the salsa by combining all the remaining ingredients in a bowl and stirring well. Cover the bowl and let stand at room temperature for 1 hour, stirring occasionally.

Let the turkey stand for 15 minutes, then slice and serve with the salsa.

TURKEY BREAST WITH APPLE-SAUSAGE DRESSING

Serves 8

1 8-pound Butterball breast of turkey, thawed if frozen

Stuffing

3 cups slightly dried white or whole-wheat bread
    cubes (3 to 4 slices, cubed and dried overnight)
1 cup crumbled, fully cooked sausage
¾ cup unpeeled diced red apple
½ cup chopped onion
½ cup chopped walnuts
½ teaspoon rubbed sage
1 teaspoon dried rosemary, crushed
¾ cup water
⅓ cup unsalted butter or margarine

Roast the turkey according to the package directions or follow the directions on pages 8–11.

Meanwhile, prepare the stuffing. Combine the bread cubes, sausage, apple, onion, walnuts, and seasonings in a large bowl. Combine the water and butter in a small saucepan and heat until the butter melts. Add the liquid to the bread mixture and toss to combine.

Put the dressing in a buttered 2-quart casserole, cover, and bake with the turkey for the last 45 minutes of roasting time.

Let the turkey stand for 10 to 15 minutes before carving. Serve with the dressing.

BREAST OF TURKEY WITH RASPBERRY-MINT GLAZE

Serves 8

Seedless raspberry jam is a treasure that you should al-ways keep in your pantry. It has many good uses, and one of the best is as a key ingredient in a glaze to brush on turkey as it roasts.

1 8-pound Butterball breast of turkey, thawed if frozen
Vegetable oil
½ cup seedless red raspberry jam
½ cup mint-apple jelly
2 teaspoons raspberry vinegar or wine vinegar
Dash of lemon pepper seasoning

Preheat the oven to 325°F. Brush the turkey breast with vegetable oil. Roast the turkey according to the package directions or follow the directions on pages 8–11.

Meanwhile, prepare the glaze. Combine the jam, jelly, vinegar, and lemon pepper in a small saucepan. Heat gently, stirring, until the jelly melts. Remove ¼ cup of the glaze and reserve the rest.

Using the ¼ cup glaze, brush the turkey several times during the last 30 minutes of roasting.

Let the turkey stand for 10 to 15 minutes before carv-ing. Slice and serve with the reserved ¾ cup raspberry glaze.

TURKEY BREAST WITH SAUTEED SQUASHES AND NOODLES

Serves 8

Here's a terrific way to use a bumper crop of summer squashes and zucchini.

---

1 3-pound frozen Butterball boneless breast of turkey, thawed if frozen
Vegetable oil
½ teaspoon rubbed sage
½ teaspoon salt
¼ teaspoon freshly ground black pepper
¼ teaspoon garlic powder
2 tablespoons unsalted butter or margarine
1 medium zucchini, thinly sliced
1 medium yellow squash, thinly sliced
6 cups hot cooked noodles
⅔ cup Marsala wine
1 cup water
1 8-ounce gravy packet (included with turkey breast)
1 cup sliced mushrooms

Preheat the oven to 325°F. Brush the turkey with oil. Combine the sage, salt, pepper, and garlic powder in a small bowl and sprinkle evenly over the turkey. Roast the turkey according to the package directions or follow the directions on pages 8–11.

When the turkey is cooked, remove from the pan and wrap in aluminum foil. Let stand for 10 to 15 minutes. Set the pan and drippings aside.

Meanwhile, melt the butter in a medium skillet over medium heat. Add the zucchini and squash and cook, stirring, until crisp-tender, about 3 minutes. Toss the squashes with the hot noodles and keep warm.

Pour the Marsala and water into the roasting pan, stirring to combine with the drippings. Stir in the contents of the gravy packet. Bring to a boil, stirring constantly. Lower the heat, add the mushrooms, and simmer for 5 minutes, stirring occasionally.

Remove the netting from the turkey. Slice the turkey and serve with squashes and noodles and gravy.

TURKEY WITH
BOMBAY CHUTNEY SAUCE

Serves 8

*Roasting a boneless turkey breast is easy and once done,
the turkey's mild flavor and succulence lend themselves
to nearly any accompaniment. Here the roasted breast is
teamed with a rich fruit chutney that is sparked with hot
red pepper. We follow the same principle in the following
recipe, serving the roasted breast with a sweet lemon
sauce (page 90).*

1 3-pound Butterball boneless breast of turkey, thawed
   if frozen

Bombay Chutney Sauce

½ cup Major Grey's mango chutney, chopped
1 8¾-ounce can sliced peaches in heavy syrup, drained
   and chopped, syrup reserved
1 8¼-ounce can crushed pineapple, drained
1 tablespoon currants
1 teaspoon cornstarch
1 teaspoon honey
¼ teaspoon crushed red pepper

Roast the turkey according to the package directions or follow the directions on pages 8–11.

Meanwhile, make the Bombay Chutney Sauce. In a medium saucepan, combine the chutney, peaches and syrup, pineapple, currants, cornstarch, honey, and red pepper. Stir until the cornstarch is blended. Bring to a boil over medium heat and cook, stirring, for 2 minutes or until thickened.

When the turkey is done, remove it from the oven and wrap in aluminum foil. Let stand for 10 to 15 minutes. Remove the netting from the turkey. Slice the turkey and serve with the warm chutney sauce.

MESQUITE-GRILLED CAJUN TURKEY

Serves 8

A popular barbecuing technique in Texas and elsewhere is called "dry rubbed," in which the food is rubbed with a boldly flavored, dry mixture made primarily from spices and herbs. Then the food is grilled. We use this technique with a boneless turkey breast, combining onion, garlic, and an array of heady spices and herbs. The turkey is grilled over mesquite, a wood found in the Southwest that imparts a subtle but unmistakable smoky flavor to the food. Backyard chefs can buy mesquite-infused charcoal briquettes or sacks of mesquite chips. If you prefer the chips, soak them for 30 minutes or so in a bucket of water and toss them on the hot fire so that they smoke as the food cooks. Add handfuls of wet chips from time to time during cooking.

---

1 3-pound Butterball boneless breast of turkey,
    thawed if frozen
Vegetable oil
1 tablespoon onion flakes
1 tablespoon garlic powder
½ teaspoon dried thyme
¼ teaspoon ground red pepper
¼ teaspoon anise seeds
¼ teaspoon ground cloves
¼ teaspoon ground allspice
1 bay leaf, crushed

Prepare a charcoal or gas grill for the indirect grilling method by following the directions on pages 12–14, using mesquite chips or coals. Brush the turkey with vegetable oil. Combine the remaining ingredients and sprinkle over the turkey.

Put the turkey on the grill. Cover the grill and cook according to the package directions or follow the directions on pages 8–11.

When the turkey is done, remove it from the grill and wrap in aluminum foil. Let stand for 10 to 15 minutes. Remove the netting and slice the turkey.

TURKEY WITH
LEMON FRUIT SAUCE

Serves 8

1 3-pound Butterball boneless breast of turkey, thawed
   if frozen

Lemon Fruit Sauce

⅓ cup fresh lemon juice
1 8¼-ounce can crushed pineapple in heavy syrup,
   undrained
½ cup golden raisins
½ cup sugar
1 3-inch cinnamon stick, broken in half
1 teaspoon grated lemon zest
1 tablespoon coarsely chopped pecans

Roast or grill the turkey according to the package directions or follow the directions on pages 8–11.

Meanwhile, prepare the lemon fruit sauce. Combine the lemon juice, undrained pineapple, raisins, sugar, and cinnamon stick in a medium saucepan. Bring to a boil over medium heat and cook for 5 to 7 minutes, stirring occasionally. Remove the pan from the heat and stir in the lemon zest and pecans. Let the sauce cool. Remove the cinnamon stick before serving.

When the turkey is done, remove it from the oven and wrap it in aluminum foil. Let stand for 10 to 15 minutes. Remove the netting from the turkey. Slice the turkey and serve with the sauce.

5

TURKEY BREAST CUTS

At Butterball we understand that everyone likes different parts of the turkey. Whatever your preference or particular mood, we have packaged a turkey cut to fit the bill. We sell meaty turkey chops, turkey cutlets and medallions, and handy breast strips that cook in a flash. All are made from succulent white meat, America's choice when it comes to turkey.

The recipes that follow for these turkey parts are simple; some can be prepared literally in minutes while others require a little more time. One more note: Throughout the book, and particularly in Chapter 6, Turkey Stews, Casseroles, and Other Easy Meals, you will find more recipes for these splendid products.

On pages 4–5 the different premium cuts are listed and how they are packaged. In the recipes we indicate how many packages of a particular cut you will need, not how much it weighs. Keep in mind that the actual weights may differ slightly from those listed here, but a few ounces one way or the other will make no difference to the outcome of the dish.

TURKEY SCALLOPINI

Serves 4

Tender, thin-cut turkey cutlets are ideal for simple sau-téing. Once cooked, we serve them with gently cooked mushrooms and a quick sherry sauce. Classic and easy. What could be better?

4 tablespoons unsalted butter or margarine
8 ounces mushrooms, sliced thin
1 1-pound package Butterball fresh boneless turkey
　　breast cutlets
¼ cup all-purpose flour
Salt
Freshly ground black pepper
¼ cup dry sherry
2 tablespoons water
Chopped parsley

Melt 2 tablespoons of the butter in a large skillet over medium heat. Add the mushrooms and cook until tender. Remove from the skillet and keep warm.

Dredge the turkey cutlets with the flour. Melt the remaining 2 tablespoons butter in the skillet. Sauté the turkey cutlets for about 2 minutes on each side or until lightly browned. Season with salt and pepper to taste. Remove from the skillet and keep warm.

Add the sherry and water to the skillet. Cook, stirring, until slightly thickened. Add the reserved mushrooms and the turkey and heat through. Sprinkle with chopped parsley before serving.

ROSEMARY-LEMON TURKEY PICCATA

Serves 4

½ cup all-purpose flour
½ teaspoon paprika
½ teaspoon dried rosemary, crushed
¼ cup fresh lemon juice
1 1-pound package Butterball fresh boneless turkey breast cutlets
3 tablespoons unsalted butter or margarine
Salt
Freshly ground black pepper

Combine the flour, paprika, and rosemary in a shallow dish. Put the lemon juice in another shallow dish. Dip the turkey cutlets in the lemon juice and then in the flour mixture until evenly coated.

Melt the butter in a large skillet over medium heat. Add the turkey cutlets and cook for 2 to 2½ minutes on each side or until lightly browned. Season with salt and pepper to taste.

ORANGE-KISSED TURKEY CUTLETS WITH HONEYED WILD RICE

Serves 4

Wild rice takes nearly an hour to cook, but the turkey cutlets require only minutes. Start the rice and then go about preparing the rest of the meal or tending to other chores. Just before dinner, cook the turkey and serve it with the honey-flavored wild rice.

1 cup wild rice
4 cups water
4 slices bacon, cooked crisp and crumbled
1 medium onion, chopped
2 cloves garlic, minced
¼ teaspoon dried thyme
¼ cup chopped parsley
2 tablespoons honey
1 tablespoon soy sauce
2 tablespoons unsalted butter or margarine
1 1-pound package Butterball fresh boneless turkey breast cutlets
1 tablespoon fresh orange juice
Salt
Freshly ground black pepper

Rinse the wild rice. Combine the rice, water, bacon, onion, 1 clove of the minced garlic, and the thyme in a medium saucepan. Bring to a boil over high heat. Reduce the heat, cover, and simmer for 45 to 50 minutes or until the rice is tender. Stir in the parsley, honey, and soy sauce. Set aside and keep warm.

Melt the butter in a large skillet over medium heat. Stir in the remaining clove of minced garlic. Add the turkey cutlets and cook for 2 to 2½ minutes on each side or until lightly browned. Spoon the orange juice over the turkey. Season with salt and pepper to taste. Serve the turkey with the rice.

TURKEY CUTLETS WITH SPRING VEGETABLES AND MUSTARD VINAIGRETTE

Serves 4

The joy of this recipe is that you can cook the fresh asparagus, green beans, and sweet new potatoes ahead of time, and then cook the cutlets when it's time to eat. If you do so, serve the dish at room temperature. The vinaigrette drizzled over the veggies makes this a delicious cross between a salad and a "full-menu" meal—perfect for a soft spring evening.

⅓ cup white wine vinegar
⅓ cup Dijon mustard
1 cup olive oil
2 tablespoons each chopped parsley and chives
1 tablespoon chopped fresh tarragon
1 tablespoon chopped scallion
1 tablespoon vegetable oil
1 tablespoon fresh lemon juice
¼ teaspoon ground red pepper
1 1-pound package Butterball fresh boneless turkey breast cutlets
1 pound asparagus spears, cooked crisp-tender
12 small new potatoes, cooked and quartered
½ pound green beans, cooked crisp-tender

To make the vinaigrette, whisk together the vinegar, mustard, olive oil, parsley, chives, tarragon, and scallion in a small bowl. Set aside.

Heat the vegetable oil in a large skillet over medium heat. Add the lemon juice and ground red pepper. Add the turkey cutlets and cook for about 2 minutes on each side or until lightly browned.

Arrange the turkey and vegetables on a serving platter or individual serving plates. Serve hot or at room temperature with the vinaigrette sprinkled over the vegetables.

TURKEY BREAST CUTLETS WITH TOMATOES AND SOUR CREAM

Serves 4

The paprika gives this one-dish meal the taste of the exotic. For the best flavor, use authentic Hungarian paprika, available in some supermarkets and most specialty stores.

---

2 tablespoons unsalted butter or margarine
1 1-pound package Butterball fresh boneless turkey breast cutlets
1 medium onion, cut into halves lengthwise and sliced
½ cup sliced carrot
1 14½-ounce can stewed tomatoes, undrained, cut up
1 teaspoon paprika
¼ teaspoon salt
Freshly ground black pepper
¼ cup sour cream

Melt the butter in a large skillet over medium heat. Add the turkey cutlets and cook for 2 to 2½ minutes on each side or until lightly browned. Remove from the skillet and set aside.

Add the onion and carrot to the skillet. Cook, stirring occasionally, for 4 to 5 minutes or until tender. Stir in the undrained tomatoes, paprika, salt, and pepper. Reduce the heat and simmer, uncovered, for 10 minutes. Stir a little of the tomato mixture into the sour cream and return the mixture to the skillet. Add the turkey to the skillet and heat through over low heat.

COCONUT-BREADED
TURKEY BREAST CUTLETS

Serves 2 to 3

Be sure you buy shredded coconut for this quick-cooking turkey supper.

1 large egg, beaten
1 tablespoon Dijon mustard
⅓ cup finely ground dried white or whole-wheat bread
    crumbs
3 tablespoons shredded coconut, chopped
1 1-pound package Butterball fresh boneless turkey
    breast cutlets
1 to 2 tablespoons unsalted butter or margarine

Combine the egg with the mustard in a shallow dish. Toss the bread crumbs and coconut together in another shallow dish. Dip the turkey cutlets in the egg mixture, then in the crumb mixture.

Melt the butter in a heavy skillet. Cook the turkey cutlets about 2½ minutes on each side.

TURKEY CUTLETS WITH MIXED PEPPER SAUTÉ

Serves 4

Mixing green, red, and yellow bell peppers in a simple sauté results in a pretty and tasty accompaniment to thin, fast-cooking turkey cutlets.

2 tablespoons vegetable oil
1 clove garlic, minced
1 red bell pepper, cut into strips
1 green bell pepper, cut into strips
1 yellow bell pepper, cut into strips
½ teaspoon lemon pepper seasoning, divided
1 1-pound package Butterball fresh boneless turkey
    breast cutlets

Heat 1 tablespoon of the oil in a medium skillet over medium heat. Add the garlic and peppers and cook for 3 to 4 minutes or until the peppers are crisp-tender. Stir in ¼ teaspoon of the lemon pepper. Keep the pepper sauté warm.

Heat the remaining 1 tablespoon oil in a large skillet over medium heat. Add the turkey cutlets and cook for 2 to 2½ minutes per side or until the meat is lightly browned. Sprinkle the turkey with the remaining ¼ teaspoon lemon pepper. Serve the turkey cutlets with the warm pepper sauté.

TURKEY CHOPS WITH RASPBERRY-MINT SAUCE

Serves 3 to 4

This straightforward recipe calls for sautéed chops served with a sweet-sour sauce made from raspberry jam, mint jelly, and a splash of vinegar. Try the same sauce with grilled turkey chops when the weather turns warm.

¼ cup seedless red raspberry jam
¼ cup mint-apple jelly
1 teaspoon raspberry vinegar or wine vinegar
1 tablespoon vegetable oil
1 1-pound package Butterball fresh turkey breast chops
Salt
Freshly ground black pepper

To make the raspberry-mint sauce, stir together the raspberry jam, mint-apple jelly, and vinegar in a small microwave-safe bowl. Microwave on High (100 percent) power for 3 minutes or until the jelly melts, stirring several times to blend. Or heat and stir in a small saucepan over medium heat until the jelly melts and the sauce is blended. Set aside.

Heat the oil in a large skillet over medium heat. Add the turkey chops and cook for 2½ to 3 minutes on each side or until lightly browned. Season with salt and pepper to taste. Serve with raspberry-mint sauce.

QUICK TURKEY RICE SKILLET

Serves 4

All-in-one meals are great for families on the go, especially when they are as nutritious and satisfying as this one made with low-fat turkey breast medallions and vitamin-rich broccoli.

¼ cup all-purpose flour
½ teaspoon salt
½ teaspoon freshly ground black pepper
¼ teaspoon poultry seasoning
1 1-pound package Butterball fresh boneless turkey breast medallions
2 tablespoons vegetable oil
2 cups water
1 tablespoon chicken bouillon granules
1 cup long-grain rice
½ cup chopped celery
Dash hot pepper sauce
1 cup frozen broccoli florets

Combine the flour, salt, ¼ teaspoon of the pepper, and the poultry seasoning in a plastic food storage bag. Add the turkey and shake to coat.

Heat the oil in a large skillet over medium heat. Add the turkey and cook, turning occasionally, for about 5 minutes or until lightly browned. Remove the turkey from the skillet and set aside.

Remove the skillet from the heat. Carefully add the water and bouillon and stir, scraping up the browned bits. Add the rice, celery, the remaining ¼ teaspoon pepper, and the pepper sauce. Put the turkey on the top. Cover and simmer over low heat for 15 minutes. Add the broccoli and continue to simmer for 5 minutes or until the liquid is absorbed.

BAKED TURKEY CHOPS
WITH STUFFING

Serves 3 to 4

For this simple oven-baked dinner, browned turkey chops are served on top of a robust stuffing and vegetable mixture.

2 tablespoons vegetable oil
1 1-pound package Butterball fresh turkey breast chops
Salt
Freshly ground black pepper
1 medium onion, chopped
2 cups shredded green cabbage
1 medium carrot, cut into julienne strips
¼ cup chopped green or red bell pepper
1½ cups water
1 6-ounce package stuffing mix with seasoning packet

Preheat the oven to 350°F. Butter an 8 × 8 × 2-inch baking dish. Heat the oil in a large skillet over medium heat. Add the turkey chops and cook for 2½ to 3 minutes on each side or until lightly browned. Season with salt and pepper to taste. Remove the chops from the skillet and set aside.

Add the onion to the skillet and cook for 4 minutes, stirring occasionally. Add the cabbage, carrot, and bell pepper and cook for 5 minutes more or until the vegetables are crisp-tender. Add the water and seasoning packet from the stuffing mix. Bring to a boil and simmer, covered, for 5 minutes. Remove from the heat.

Stir the stuffing into the vegetable mixture. Spoon the mixture into the prepared baking pan. Put the turkey chops on top of the stuffing, cover the pan with aluminum foil, and bake for 20 minutes or until hot.

SIX-MINUTE TURKEY SQUASH STIR-FRY

Serves 4

Summer squash, snow peas, green bell peppers, and cheerful cherry tomatoes mingle with small strips of juicy turkey in this last-minute stir-fry. Serve it over rice or spoon it into a flour tortilla.

---

1 1-pound package Butterball fresh boneless turkey
   breast strips
½ teaspoon garlic powder
½ teaspoon paprika
3 tablespoons unsalted butter or margarine
1 medium yellow squash, sliced thin
1 small green bell pepper, cut into 1-inch pieces
¼ pound fresh snow peas
½ teaspoon Italian seasoning
8 to 10 cherry tomatoes, cut in half
Salt
Freshly ground black pepper

Combine the turkey strips, garlic powder, and paprika in a medium bowl.

Melt 2 tablespoons of the butter in a large skillet or wok over medium-high heat. Stir-fry the turkey for about 3 minutes or until the meat is no longer pink. Remove the turkey from the pan and keep warm.

Melt the remaining tablespoon of butter in the skillet. Add the squash, bell pepper, snow peas, and Italian seasoning. Stir-fry for about 3 minutes or until the vegetables are crisp-tender. Stir in the reserved turkey and tomatoes. Season with salt and pepper to taste and heat through.

BARBECUED TURKEY STRIPS

Serves 4 to 5

Use your favorite store-bought barbecue sauce and cranberry-raspberry sauce for the barbecue here. Flour tortillas are a little larger than corn tortillas, and they have a white, powdery appearance and milder flavor.

1 tablespoon vegetable oil
1 medium onion, chopped
½ cup chopped red bell pepper
1 1-pound package Butterball fresh boneless turkey breast strips
1 cup barbecue sauce
⅓ cup cranberry-raspberry sauce
4 to 5 flour tortillas, heated

Heat the oil in a large skillet over medium heat. Add the onion and pepper and cook for about 5 minutes, stirring occasionally, or until crisp-tender. Remove the vegetables with a slotted spoon and set aside.

Add the turkey strips to the skillet. Cook for 4 minutes, stirring occasionally, or until no longer pink.

Combine the barbecue sauce with the cranberry-raspberry sauce in a small bowl. Add the sauce mixture and the vegetables to the skillet. Cover and simmer over low heat for 5 minutes or until hot. Serve the barbecued turkey strips wrapped in tortillas.

6

TURKEY STEWS, CASSEROLES, AND OTHER EASY MEALS

No doubt you will turn to this chapter time and again as it is chock-full of easy, fast, and delicious meals perfect for family suppers and weekend lunches. Some of the recipes rely on leftover or already-cooked meat; others call for ground turkey. Most can be easily prepared and cooked in an hour or less.

Keep in mind that our turkey products such as ground meat and turkey medallions are packaged in sizes of varying weight. When a recipe calls for a one-pound package of, say, ground turkey, do not worry if it is not exactly one pound—a little more or less will not make a difference in the outcome of the recipe. Turkey is, you will quickly discover, amazingly versatile, particularly with the wide and tempting assortment of Butterball turkey products available in the meat department of the supermarket.

TURKEY CURRY FAVORS

Makes 48 appetizers;
serves 6 to 8 as a main course

These flavorful little balls of cooked turkey coated in toasted almonds and coconut are great party fare, especially as they can be made well in advance. They are also delicious served with sliced apples, pears, and other fruits for a light lunch. Toast the slivered almonds and coconut separately. Both should be spread in a single layer in a shallow pan and toasted in a 350°F. oven for 5 to 10 minutes until lightly browned. It is important to stir the coconut three or four times and to shake the pan holding the almonds during toasting. And let them cool before using.

1 cup slivered almonds, lightly toasted
1 cup shredded sweetened coconut, lightly toasted
3 cups chopped cooked Butterball turkey
3 scallions, trimmed and chopped
8 ounces cream cheese, softened
½ cup Major Grey's mango chutney
2 teaspoons curry powder
1 teaspoon ground ginger
Salt
1½ cups (6 ounces) shredded sharp cheddar cheese
2 teaspoons grated lime zest

Put the toasted almonds and coconut in a food processor and process until finely chopped. Transfer to a shallow dish (such as a pie plate) and set aside.

Put the turkey and scallions in the food processor and process until minced. Remove and set aside. Next put the cream cheese, chutney, curry powder, ginger, and salt to taste in the food processor and process until blended. Then add the minced turkey and scallions, the cheddar cheese and lime zest. Pulse briefly just to combine. Chill the turkey mixture at least 1 hour.

Using your hands, roll the turkey mixture into balls about 1 inch in diameter. Roll each ball in the almond/coconut mixture until evenly coated. Put the balls on a flat tray, cover, and refrigerate for at least 1 hour before serving.

DAY-AFTER TURKEY DIVAN

Serves 8 to 10

Sun-dried tomatoes are no longer relegated to the shelves of gourmet food shops. These days they are quite easy to find in the local supermarket. If you have not yet tried them, you will discover their rich flavor and pleasingly chewy texture a welcome addition to many dishes. They are very different from canned tomatoes, so do not substitute one for the other. If you cannot find the tomatoes, omit them. Here, we team oil-packed sun-dried tomatoes with leftover turkey, broccoli, and pasta in an easy-to-make, quick casserole.

2 tablespoons olive oil
1 bunch scallions, trimmed and finely chopped
5 cloves garlic, minced
24 sun-dried tomatoes packed in oil, drained, and cut into slivers
12 ounces vermicelli
1 large bunch broccoli, tender stalks and florets cooked until just tender
4 cups chopped cooked Butterball turkey
¾ cup (3 ounces) crumbled blue cheese
5 large eggs
2½ cups half-and-half
1 tablespoon dried tarragon
1½ teaspoons salt
1 teaspoon freshly ground black pepper
½ cup dried bread crumbs tossed with 2 tablespoons melted unsalted butter or margarine

Preheat the oven to 350°F. Butter a shallow 2½-quart casserole or lasagne pan.

Heat the olive oil in a small heavy skillet over medium-high heat. Add the scallions and garlic and cook, stirring, for 3 to 4 minutes or until softened. Add the sun-dried tomatoes and cook for 1 minute more.

Cook the vermicelli in boiling salted water according to package directions until just tender. Drain the vermicelli. Combine the drained pasta with the cooked vegetables in a large bowl. Gently stir in the broccoli, turkey, and blue cheese.

Beat the eggs with the half-and-half until well combined. Stir in the tarragon, salt, and pepper. Pour the mixture over the pasta mixture, combining well. Turn into the prepared casserole and sprinkle the buttered bread crumbs over the top. Bake for 40 to 45 minutes, until lightly crusted and hot.

BAKED TURKEY TOSTADA

Serves 3 to 4

Relying on pantry ingredients—those you most likely have on hand—these spicy little snacks use refrigerated biscuit dough and take only minutes to bake. Your kids will love them.

1¾ cups chopped Butterball Slice 'N Serve barbecue
    seasoned breast of turkey (about 9 ounces)
⅔ cup chunky salsa
Yellow cornmeal
1 4½-ounce can refrigerated buttermilk biscuits
    (6 biscuits)
Shredded cheddar cheese
Shredded lettuce
Sour cream

Preheat the oven to 400°F. Butter a baking sheet. Combine the turkey and salsa in a bowl and set aside.

Sprinkle a work surface with cornmeal. Separate the biscuit dough into 6 biscuits and roll each into a 4-inch circle. Turn each biscuit over to coat both sides with cornmeal.

Put the biscuits on the baking sheet. Spoon the turkey mixture onto the biscuits and bake for 10 to 12 minutes. Serve topped with cheese, lettuce, and sour cream.

SUMMERTIME VEGGIE AND TURKEY GRILL PACKETS

Serves 4

You will need heavy-duty aluminum foil and about 15 minutes of grill time for this easy meal. Anything else? Perhaps a green salad and a loaf of French bread.

1 pound Butterball Slice 'N Serve skinless mesquite smoked breast of turkey, cut into 1½-inch strips (about 3 cups)
1½ cups thinly sliced yellow squash
1½ cups thinly sliced zucchini
½ cup julienne strips of red bell pepper
3 tablespoons grated Parmesan cheese
½ teaspoon dried basil
Dash of lemon pepper seasoning

Prepare a charcoal or gas grill.

Combine all the ingredients in a large bowl and stir well to combine. Cut 4 large sheets of heavy-duty aluminum foil. Put one-fourth of the mixture on each sheet. Bring the foil up and over the turkey mixture and double-fold the edges to seal each packet.

Put the foil packets on the grill over medium heat for 15 minutes or until hot, turning once. Serve in the foil packets. Alternatively, heat the packets in a preheated 375°F. oven for 15 minutes, turning them once.

TURKEY CALZONES

Serves 4

These pizza pie packets are made from pizza dough, readily available in the refrigerator sections of most supermarkets.

1 tablespoon vegetable oil
¾ cup sliced mushrooms
⅓ cup chopped green bell pepper
⅓ cup chopped onion
1 10-ounce package refrigerated pizza crust dough
¼ cup pizza or spaghetti sauce
1 cup chopped Butterball Slice 'N Serve skinless barbe-
    cue seasoned breast of turkey (about 5 ounces)
1 cup (4 ounces) shredded mozzarella cheese
¼ cup grated Parmesan cheese

Preheat the oven to 400°F. Butter a baking sheet.

Heat the oil in a medium skillet over medium heat. Add the mushrooms, bell pepper, and onion and cook, stirring occasionally, until softened. Set the vegetables aside.

Unroll the pizza dough and cut into 4 equal rectangles. Press each piece into a 6-inch square. Spread 1 tablespoon pizza sauce in a triangle over half of each dough square to within ½ inch of the edge. Top the sauce evenly with some of the vegetable mixture, turkey, and cheeses. Moisten the edges of the dough with water. Carefully fold the dough over the filling to form a triangle. Pinch the edges firmly to seal.

Put the calzones on the baking sheet. Pierce the top of each with a fork or knife to allow steam to escape. Bake for 12 to 15 minutes or until golden brown.

SMOKED TURKEY FETTUCCINE

Serves 4 to 5

Pretty green spinach fettuccine is perfect for chunky white sauces, such as this one made with smoked turkey and mushrooms. Thinner pasta would not hold the sauce as well.

8 ounces uncooked spinach fettuccine
3 tablespoons unsalted butter or margarine
3 tablespoons all-purpose flour
1 cup milk
1 cup chicken broth
¼ cup grated Parmesan cheese
¼ teaspoon salt
Dash of ground white pepper
2 cups chopped Butterball Slice 'N Serve skinless hickory smoked breast of turkey (about 10 ounces)
1 2½-ounce jar sliced mushrooms, drained

Cook the fettuccine according to package directions while preparing the sauce.

Meanwhile, melt the butter in a medium saucepan over low heat. Stir in the flour and cook, stirring, for 1 to 2 minutes. Increase the heat to medium and gradually stir in the milk and broth. Continue to cook, stirring, until the sauce is thickened. Add the cheese, salt, pepper, turkey, and mushrooms and continue to cook, stirring occasionally, until the turkey is hot. Serve the turkey and mushroom sauce over the cooked fettuccine.

CURRIED TURKEY KABOBS

Serves 4

Low-fat yogurt is a wonderful ingredient for marinades. It adds tang and texture. The combination of yogurt, lemon, and garlic is a classic in many Middle Eastern and Asian cuisines.

¾ cup plain low-fat yogurt
2 tablespoons finely chopped onion
1 clove garlic, crushed
1 tablespoon fresh lemon juice
1 teaspoon curry powder
¼ teaspoon salt
⅛ teaspoon ground cloves
1 1-pound package Butterball fresh boneless turkey breast medallions
3 cups hot cooked rice
Major Grey's mango chutney

Preheat the broiler.

Combine the yogurt, onion, garlic, lemon juice, curry powder, salt, and cloves in a medium bowl. Add the turkey and stir gently to coat with the yogurt mixture.

Thread the turkey medallions onto four 10-inch metal skewers, leaving a little space between each piece. Spoon the remaining yogurt mixture over the turkey, if desired. Broil 4 inches from the heat for 18 to 20 minutes, turning several times. Serve the turkey kabobs with hot rice and chutney.

GRILLED THAI TURKEY KABOBS

Serves 4

It is important that all food to be threaded on skewers for grilling, such as the turkey, peppers, and pineapple for these kabobs, be cut to a fairly uniform size so that they cook evenly and are large enough to stay on the skewers during cooking. If you prefer, substitute orange juice for the orange-flavored liqueur.

1 pound Butterball Slice 'N Serve hickory smoked
 breast of turkey, cut into 1¼-inch pieces
 (about 3 cups)
1 large green bell pepper, cut into 1¼-inch pieces
1 large red bell pepper, cut into 1¼-inch pieces
½ medium pineapple, cut into 1¼-inch chunks
1 8-ounce package pitted dates
2 teaspoons grated fresh ginger
1 teaspoon minced garlic
⅓ cup Triple Sec or other orange-flavored liqueur
⅓ cup fresh lime juice
1 tablespoon dark oriental sesame oil
1 tablespoon vegetable oil
1 tablespoon soy sauce
¼ teaspoon ground red pepper

Put the turkey, peppers, pineapple, and dates in a shallow glass or nonreactive bowl. Combine the remaining ingredients in a small bowl and pour over the turkey mixture. Cover and refrigerate for at least 1½ hours, turning the turkey mixture several times.

Prepare a charcoal or gas grill. Drain the marinade into a saucepan and bring to a boil over medium heat. Assemble the kabobs on four 12-inch metal skewers, alternating the ingredients. Grill the kabobs over medium heat for 15 to 18 minutes, turning frequently and basting with the warm marinade. Alternatively, preheat the broiler and broil the kabobs 4 inches from the heat for 15 to 18 minutes, turning several times and basting with the marinade.

MEXICAN TURKEY MINI PIZZAS

Serves 4

When you begin using ground turkey, you will find it as versatile as other ground meats, and far less fatty. These mini pizzas are just one delicious idea.

Yellow cornmeal
Vegetable oil
1 10-ounce package refrigerated pizza crust dough
1 1-pound package Butterball fresh ground turkey
1 clove garlic, minced
1 cup chunky salsa
¼ teaspoon ground cumin
1 cup canned refried beans
1 tomato, chopped
Shredded Monterey Jack cheese
Sliced scallions

Preheat the oven to 425°F. Butter a baking sheet and sprinkle with cornmeal.

Unroll the pizza dough and press into a 13 × 10-inch rectangle on the prepared baking sheet. Brush lightly with oil and sprinkle with cornmeal. Cut the dough into four 6½ × 5-inch rectangles. Prick the rectangles all over with a fork. Bake 5 to 8 minutes or until the crust just begins to brown. Set aside. Do not turn the oven off.

Heat 1 tablespoon oil in a 10-inch skillet over medium heat. Add the turkey and garlic, breaking up the turkey with a wooden spoon, and cook until no longer pink. Stir in the salsa and cumin and continue to cook, stirring occasionally, until the liquid evaporates.

To assemble the pizzas, spread each with ¼ cup beans to within ½ inch of the edge. Top each with about ¾ cup of the turkey mixture. Bake for 8 to 10 minutes. Sprinkle with chopped tomato, cheese, and scallions before serving.

LEMON TURKEY STIR-FRY

Serves 4

After removing the zest of the lemon, the colored part of the skin without any of the bitter white pith attached, use the fruit for the fresh lemon juice. Thin-skinned, heavy lemons yield the most juice.

½ cup chicken broth
3 tablespoons soy sauce
1 teaspoon grated lemon zest
3 tablespoons fresh lemon juice
1 teaspoon sugar
1 tablespoon cornstarch
1 tablespoon vegetable oil
1 cup sliced carrots, cut on the diagonal
1 6-ounce package frozen snow peas, thawed
1 clove garlic, minced
1 1-pound package Butterball fresh boneless turkey breast strips
3 scallions, halved lengthwise and cut into 1-inch pieces, optional
3 cups hot cooked rice

Combine the broth, soy sauce, lemon zest, lemon juice, sugar, and cornstarch in a small bowl. Set aside.

Heat the vegetable oil in a large skillet over medium heat. Add the carrots and stir-fry for 30 to 40 seconds. Add the snow peas and garlic and stir-fry for 30 seconds. Remove the vegetables from the skillet with a slotted spoon and set aside.

Add the turkey to the skillet and cook, stirring occasionally, for about 4 minutes or until no longer pink. Add the reserved broth mixture. Bring to a boil and cook, stirring, until thickened. Stir in the scallions and the reserved vegetables. Serve over hot rice.

HERB-SEASONED
TURKEY PATTIES

Serves 4

Ground turkey is naturally low in fat, which explains why it needs a little oil in the pan as it cooks. Unlike beef and pork, it releases very little fat as it cooks.

1 1-pound package Butterball fresh ground turkey
2 tablespoons finely ground dry white or whole-wheat bread crumbs
2 tablespoons finely chopped onion
¼ teaspoon dried thyme
¼ teaspoon lemon pepper seasoning
¼ teaspoon salt
1 tablespoon vegetable oil

Put the turkey, bread crumbs, onion, thyme, pepper, and salt in a bowl and mix until well combined. Shape into 4 patties about ½ inch thick.

Heat the oil in a skillet over medium heat. Cook the patties 5 to 6 minutes to a side or until the meat is no longer pink.

TURKEY BURRITOS

Serves 4

½ cup salsa picante
8 ounces cooked Butterball boneless breast of turkey,
    cut into ¼-inch-thick julienne strips
    (about 1½ cups)
1 16-ounce can refried beans
8 flour tortillas
½ cup chopped tomatoes
¾ cup (3 ounces) shredded cheddar or Monterey Jack
    cheese
Guacamole
Sour cream

Pour ⅓ cup of the salsa over the turkey strips. Cover and marinate in the refrigerator for 1 hour.

Preheat the oven to 350°F.

Heat the beans with the remaining salsa in a small saucepan, stirring constantly. Heat the tortillas according to package directions.

Spoon the bean mixture down the center of each tortilla. Top with the marinated turkey strips, tomatoes, and cheese. Fold one edge of each tortilla over the filling. Fold in the sides and roll. Put the filled tortillas on a baking sheet, seam side down, and bake for 10 minutes or until the cheese is melted. Top each burrito with guacamole and sour cream before serving.

TURKEY WILD RICE CASSEROLE

Serves 5 to 6

1 6-ounce package long grain and wild rice mix
¾ pound cooked Butterball breast of turkey, cut into
    ½-inch pieces (about 2 cups)
1 2½-ounce jar sliced mushrooms, drained
¼ cup coarsely grated carrot
¼ cup finely chopped broccoli
1 cup (4 ounces) shredded Swiss cheese
¾ cup half-and-half
2 tablespoons dry sherry
¼ teaspoon freshly ground black pepper
Grated Parmesan cheese
2 tablespoons sliced scallions

Preheat the oven to 350°F. Prepare the rice according to package directions.

Combine the cooked rice, turkey, mushrooms, carrot, broccoli, and ½ cup of the Swiss cheese in a 2-quart baking dish. Combine the half-and-half, sherry, and pepper and pour over the turkey mixture, folding gently. Sprinkle the remaining Swiss and Parmesan cheeses over the top. Bake for 30 to 40 minutes or until the casserole is hot and bubbly. Garnish with the scallions before serving.

TURKEY SATAY

Serves 4

Throughout Southeast Asia, satay, marinated cubes of meat threaded on skewers, are sold by street vendors on almost every corner and pedestrians stop to snack on the freshly grilled meat at any hour. We have re-created the dish and flavored it with a rich, slightly spicy nutty sauce for the home kitchen. Use creamy peanut butter, not chunky, and be sure you use ground coriander and not coriander seeds, which are extremely strong in taste.

¾ cup smooth peanut butter
¾ cup heavy cream
1 tablespoon brown sugar
3 cloves garlic, minced
1 tablespoon finely chopped onion
1¼ teaspoons ground coriander
1 teaspoon ground cumin
½ teaspoon dry mustard
½ teaspoon crushed red pepper
¾ pound cooked Butterball breast of turkey, cut into
    1-inch cubes (about 2½ cups)

Preheat the broiler.

Put all the ingredients except the turkey in a food processor or blender and process until smooth.

Thread the turkey cubes onto 4 metal skewers and broil 4 to 5 inches from the heat for 2 to 3 minutes on each side or until the turkey is heated through. Serve the turkey hot with the sauce at room temperature.

TURKEY FAJITAS

Serves 4

Fajitas have become extremely popular in the Southwest and their fame is spreading to the north, too. The tortilla and meat "sandwiches" make a wonderful light supper or lunch.

2 tablespoons soy sauce
1 tablespoon fresh lime juice
¼ cup coarsely chopped onion
¼ cup coarsely chopped green bell pepper
2 cloves garlic, minced
¼ to ½ teaspoon crushed red pepper flakes
1 pound cooked Butterball boneless breast of turkey,
    cut into ½ × ¼-inch strips (about 3 cups)
1 tablespoon vegetable oil
1 12-ounce jar salsa picante, mild or hot
4 flour tortillas
Refried beans
Chopped tomatoes
Shredded lettuce

Combine the soy sauce, lime juice, onion, green pepper, garlic, and red pepper flakes in a small bowl. Put the turkey in a glass or nonreactive dish. Pour the marinade over it, cover, and refrigerate for 2 to 3 hours.

Heat the oil in a skillet over medium-high heat. Add the marinated turkey mixture and stir-fry for 3 to 5 minutes. Stir in the salsa and simmer until the mixture is heated through. Remove from the heat.

Spoon some of the turkey mixture down the center of each tortilla and roll the tortilla up. Serve the fajitas with refried beans, tomatoes, and lettuce.

TURKEY STEW WITH DUMPLINGS

Serves 6

Soft dumplings simmered atop a flavorful stew have long been an American favorite. We use a simple buttermilk baking mix for the dumplings, which makes this hearty casserole a breeze to prepare.

2 tablespoons unsalted butter or margarine
1 medium onion, sliced
2 stalks celery, sliced
3 cups chopped cooked Butterball turkey
    (about 1 pound)
2 cups coarsely chopped green cabbage
1 16-ounce can tomatoes, undrained and cut up
1 15½-ounce can kidney beans, undrained
2 13¾-ounce cans chicken broth
1 cup water
2 tablespoons sugar
1½ teaspoons dried marjoram
1 teaspoon salt
2 cups buttermilk baking mix
⅔ cup milk

Melt the butter in a large saucepan over medium heat. Add the onion and celery and cook, stirring occasionally, until crisp-tender. Add the turkey, cabbage, tomatoes, beans, broth, water, sugar, marjoram, and salt. Cover and simmer for 25 minutes or until the cabbage is tender.

Combine the baking mix with the milk and stir until a soft dough forms. Drop the dough by spoonfuls onto the hot stew to make 12 dumplings. Cover and simmer for 15 minutes. Serve the stew in bowls.

TURKEY-VEGETABLE STIR-FRY

Serves 4

3 tablespoons vegetable oil
2 medium carrots, cut into thin diagonal slices
¼ cup peanuts
¾ pound cooked Butterball boneless breast of turkey,
    cut into ½ × ¼-inch strips (about 2 cups)
1 6-ounce package frozen pea pods, thawed
2 teaspoons cornstarch
⅔ cup water
2 tablespoons dry sherry
2 tablespoons soy sauce
¼ teaspoon dark oriental sesame oil
1 clove garlic, minced
3 cups hot cooked rice

Heat the vegetable oil in a large skillet over medium heat. Add the carrots and stir-fry until crisp-tender. Add the peanuts and cook, stirring, for 1 minute. Add the turkey and pea pods and cook, stirring, for 2 to 3 minutes.

Mix the cornstarch with the water in a small bowl. Add the sherry, soy sauce, sesame oil, garlic, and cornstarch mixture to the skillet. Continue to cook, stirring, for 2 to 3 minutes or until the sauce thickens and the mixture is heated through. Serve over hot cooked rice.

SWEET-AND-SOUR TURKEY ON RICE

Serves 6 to 8

1 20-ounce can pineapple chunks, packed in heavy
   syrup
1 6-ounce can pineapple juice (¾ cup)
¼ cup packed brown sugar
1½ tablespoons cornstarch
¼ cup white wine vinegar
2 tablespoons ketchup
¼ to ½ teaspoon ground cinnamon
½ teaspoon salt
2 cups chopped cooked Butterball turkey
   (about 10 ounces)
1 medium green bell pepper, cut into strips
1 tomato, cut into wedges
5 cups hot cooked rice

Drain the pineapple, reserving the syrup. Combine the
syrup, pineapple juice, brown sugar, cornstarch, vinegar, ketchup, cinnamon, and salt in a large saucepan.
Cook, stirring, over medium heat until thickened. Stir in
the turkey, pineapple chunks, green pepper, and tomato
and cook, stirring occasionally, for 10 minutes or until
hot. Serve over hot cooked rice.

TURKEY POT PIE

Serves 6

As with many of our recipes, we have simplified this one for pot pie by using refrigerated pie dough. The dough is easy to find, easy to work with, and tastes just right with this savory stew.

1½ cups peeled diced sweet potatoes
2 cups broccoli florets or 1 10-ounce package frozen chopped broccoli, thawed
1 cup frozen pearl onions, thawed
2½ cups chopped cooked Butterball turkey (about ¾ pound)
¼ cup chopped parsley
2 tablespoons unsalted butter or margarine
3 tablespoons cornstarch
¾ to 1½ teaspoons chopped fresh rosemary or ¼ to ½ teaspoon dried rosemary, crushed
¼ teaspoon freshly ground black pepper
Dash of ground allspice
1¾ cups chicken broth
¼ cup dry white wine
1 refrigerated pie crust
1 teaspoon all-purpose flour
1 large egg, beaten with 1 tablespoon water

Put the sweet potatoes in a medium saucepan. Add water to cover, bring to a boil, and cook, covered, for 4 minutes. Add the broccoli and onions to the pan and cook, covered, for 1 to 2 minutes more or until the vegetables are crisp-tender. Drain well. Turn the vegetable mixture into a shallow oval or square 2-quart baking dish. Stir in the turkey and parsley.

Using the same saucepan, melt the butter over medium heat. Stir in the cornstarch, rosemary, pepper, and allspice. Gradually stir in the chicken broth and wine and continue to cook, stirring, until thickened. Pour the sauce over the turkey mixture in the baking dish and stir gently to combine. Set aside.

Preheat the oven to 375°F.

Unfold the pie crust. Peel off 1 sheet of plastic. Sprinkle the pastry with the flour and roll the dough out to fit the filled baking dish. Put the pastry crust, floured-side down, over the top of the dish. Trim the edges and press the pastry around the edges of the dish. Cut a slash in the center of the crust as a steam vent. Brush the pastry with the beaten egg.

Put the dish on a baking sheet and bake for 30 to 35 minutes or until the crust is golden brown. Let the pie stand for 5 minutes before serving.

TURKEY SPOON BREAD

Serves 6

Spoon breads are related to soufflés, but they are far less fragile. Like soufflés, they are lightened with beaten egg whites and rise to puffy heights in the oven. They also should be eaten immediately after baking. Called spoon breads because they are meant to be spooned right from the dish onto the waiting plate, they have long been popular in the South and make a tasty one-dish meal.

3 cups milk, divided
1 cup yellow cornmeal
4 tablespoons unsalted butter or margarine
1 tablespoon sugar
1½ teaspoons baking powder
¼ teaspoon salt
¼ teaspoon ground red pepper
2 cups finely chopped cooked Butterball turkey
    (about 10 ounces)
1 cup whole kernel corn, fresh or frozen and thawed,
    drained well
½ cup finely chopped scallions
4 large eggs, separated
Red pepper relish or salsa, optional

Preheat the oven to 325°F. Butter a 2-quart soufflé dish or casserole.

Combine 2¼ cups of the milk with the cornmeal in a 3-quart saucepan. Cook over medium heat, stirring constantly, for 8 to 10 minutes or until the mixture is very thick and pulls away from the sides of the pan.

Reduce the heat to low. Stir in the remaining ¾ cup milk, butter, sugar, baking powder, salt, and red pepper. Cook, stirring, for about 2 minutes or until the butter is melted. Remove the pan from the heat. Add the turkey, corn, and scallions and fold them in gently. Set aside.

Beat the egg whites in a medium bowl until stiff peaks form. In another medium bowl, beat the egg yolks until thick and lemon-colored. Stir 1 cup of the hot turkey mixture into the beaten yolks and then combine with the turkey mixture in the pan. Gently fold the egg whites into the turkey mixture.

Turn the mixture into the prepared dish. Bake for 1 to 1¼ hours or until a knife inserted near the center comes out clean. Serve the spoon bread immediately, with red pepper relish or salsa, if desired.

TURKEY HASH

Serves 6

For years hash was a regular item in diners and coffee shops—and a way to utilize leftover meat. Hash nearly always includes potatoes and onions and frequently is served with a fried egg on top.

1½ pounds small new red potatoes, cut into pieces
3 tablespoons unsalted butter or margarine
1 large onion, chopped
1 large green bell pepper, coarsely chopped
1 large red or yellow bell pepper, coarsely chopped
2 large stalks celery, sliced
1 tablespoon poultry seasoning
1 tablespoon Worcestershire sauce
¼ teaspoon salt
¼ teaspoon freshly ground black pepper
2 cups chopped cooked Butterball turkey
    (about 10 ounces)
¾ cup half-and-half or milk
4 large eggs
3 tablespoons finely chopped chives or scallions
Coarsely ground black pepper

Put the potato pieces in a large saucepan, cover with cold water, and bring to a boil. Cook, covered, for 10 to 12 minutes or until just tender. Drain the potatoes and set aside.

Melt the butter in a large heavy skillet over medium heat. Add the onion, bell peppers, celery, poultry seasoning, Worcestershire sauce, salt, and pepper. Cook, stirring, for 5 to 7 minutes or until the vegetables are crisp-tender. Stir in the turkey, cooked potatoes, and half-and-half and continue to cook, covered, over low heat for about 10 minutes or until the mixture is hot.

Meanwhile, fry the eggs in another skillet. Serve the hash topped with the fried eggs, sprinkled with chives and coarsely ground pepper.

SLICED TURKEY WITH CURRIED FRUIT SAUCE

Serves 4

This and the following recipe with creamy pecan-Dijon sauce are good ways to serve leftover roast turkey or boneless turkey.

---

1 11-ounce can mandarin oranges
1 tablespoon cornstarch
1 tablespoon packed brown sugar
1 teaspoon chicken bouillon granules
½ teaspoon curry powder
⅛ teaspoon ground ginger
½ cup seedless green grapes, cut in half
8 slices hot cooked Butterball turkey

Drain the juice from the oranges and reserve. Add water to make 1½ cups.

Combine the cornstarch, brown sugar, bouillon granules, curry powder, and ginger in a small saucepan. Gradually stir in the reserved liquid and cook, stirring, over medium-high heat until thickened. Stir in the oranges and grapes.

Serve the sauce over the hot sliced turkey.

SLICED TURKEY WITH CREAMY PECAN-DIJON SAUCE

Serves 4

1 tablespoon unsalted butter or margarine
2 tablespoons peeled, chopped shallots
1 clove garlic, minced
1 cup heavy cream
⅓ cup dry sherry
½ cup coarsely chopped pecans
½ cup seedless red or green grapes, cut in half
¼ cup Dijon mustard
8 slices hot cooked Butterball turkey

Melt the butter in a medium skillet over medium-high heat. Add the shallots and garlic and cook, stirring occasionally, until softened. Stir in the cream and sherry. Continue to cook, stirring, for about 4 minutes or until the sauce is slightly thickened. Do not allow the sauce to boil. Stir in the pecans, grapes, and mustard.

Serve the sauce over the hot sliced turkey.

TURKEY CASSOULET

Serves 8

Cassoulet is a traditional French one-dish meal that always includes meat, sausage, and beans.

1 3-pound Butterball boneless turkey
2 15½-ounce cans great Northern beans, drained
1 15-ounce can tomato sauce
¼ cup chopped onion
2 cloves garlic, minced
1 teaspoon fennel seed
¼ teaspoon freshly ground black pepper
½ pound fully cooked Polish smoked sausage, cut into
    ½-inch pieces
6 slices cooked bacon, cut into 1-inch pieces

Preheat the oven to 325°F. Roast the turkey according to package directions or follow the directions on pages 8–11.

Meanwhile, combine the remaining ingredients in a 2-quart casserole. Cover and bake with the turkey for the last hour.

Wrap the turkey in aluminum foil and let stand 10 to 15 minutes before slicing. Remove the netting from the turkey. Slice and serve the slices over the bean mixture.

7

TURKEY SOUPS

Making soup is a satisfying pastime if ever there was one. And the results provide your family and friends with a nourishing, delicious meal that need never strain the weekly budget. For the most part, our soups were developed with leftovers in mind, but if you do not have leftover turkey in the refrigerator, consider buying a Butterball Slice 'N Serve turkey breast to use for soups, sandwiches, and salads.

We know there are days when you may yearn for a bowl of steaming hot soup but cannot find the time or summon the energy to do more than open a can. Before reaching for the can opener, read through the recipes on these pages. Some soups in this chapter can be ready in no time. Start with a can of chicken broth, then add frozen vegetables, herbs, and cooked turkey. In mere minutes, you have homemade soup.

If you have time, we urge you to make your own turkey broth. The first recipe in the chapter is for full-flavored Turkey Frame Broth, made from the turkey carcass. One of the wonderful things about homemade broth is that it freezes well; you can simply take a container of frozen homemade broth from the freezer and use it instead.

TURKEY FRAME BROTH

Makes about 8 cups

Making your own turkey broth is so easy and adds such good flavor to soups, sauces, and gravies, you will wonder why you never tried it before. This recipe makes a half gallon of broth, which may sound like a lot, but because it freezes beautifully, it makes sense to make large quantities. Chill the broth in the refrigerator before freezing it—do not leave it at room temperature—and freeze it in handy-sized plastic containers to use as needed.

1 roasted Butterball turkey carcass, preferably with
    some meat
3 stalks celery, cut into 4 pieces
1 carrot, cut into 4 pieces
1 onion, quartered
2 cloves garlic, cut in half
1 bay leaf
1½ teaspoons salt
10 black peppercorns
⅛ teaspoon paprika
10 cups water

Break up the turkey carcass and put the pieces in a heavy 4-quart saucepan or stockpot. Add the remaining ingredients. Bring to a boil over high heat. Reduce the heat to low, cover, and simmer for 2 hours.

Remove the carcass from the pan and set aside to cool. When cool enough to handle, remove the turkey meat from the bones and reserve for another use, if desired. Discard the carcass. Strain the broth and discard the vegetables and seasonings. Use the broth for soups, gravies, and sauces.

TURKEY AND SAUSAGE GUMBO

Serves 14 to 16

Gumbo, a cross between soup and stew, is a regional specialty of Louisiana. The chunky soup can be made with a variety of vegetables, meats, or seafood, and we think coarsely chopped, cooked turkey is one of the best choices. Andouille sausage is classic New Orleans fare, but any spicy pork sausage will do. The okra and the filé powder both give gumbo its distinctive thickness, and in some recipes one may be omitted in favor of the other. We use filé powder (pronounced FEE-lay) to strengthen the thickening power of frozen okra. Be sure not to let the soup boil after the filé is added or it will lose its thickening abilities.

⅓ pound sliced bacon, cut into ½-inch dice
1 large onion, chopped
1 bunch scallions, trimmed and chopped
1 red bell pepper, chopped
1 yellow bell pepper, chopped
3 stalks celery, diced
4 cloves garlic, minced
2 jalapeño peppers, seeded and finely chopped
7 cups Turkey Frame Broth (preceding recipe) or canned chicken broth
2 28-ounce cans plum tomatoes, undrained
2 10-ounce packages frozen sliced okra, thawed
1 10-ounce package frozen whole kernel corn, thawed
1½ pounds andouille or other spicy pork sausage, cut into ½-inch pieces

2 teaspoons dried thyme
4 cups chopped cooked Butterball turkey
Salt
Freshly ground black pepper
1 tablespoon gumbo filé powder
7 to 8 cups hot cooked rice

Put the bacon, onion, scallions, bell peppers, celery, garlic, and jalapeño peppers in a large heavy saucepan over medium heat. Cook, stirring occasionally, for 15 to 20 minutes or until the vegetables are very tender.

Add the broth, undrained tomatoes, okra, corn, andouille, and thyme. Bring to a boil and simmer, partially covered, for 1 hour. Stir in the turkey and season with salt and pepper to taste. The soup may be prepared up to this point and refrigerated for a day or two or frozen for up to a month.

When ready to serve the gumbo, heat the soup to just below simmering and stir in the gumbo filé powder. Do not allow the soup to boil after the filé is added.

Serve the gumbo over mounds of rice in large shallow soup bowls.

TURKEY WILD RICE
PUMPKIN SOUP

Serves 6 to 8

This is a wonderful soup to make during the Thanksgiving weekend as it relies on leftover turkey and wild rice, incorporating the best flavors from Thursday's feast. Pick up an extra can of unsweetened pumpkin purée when doing the holiday shopping and plan on serving the warm thick soup over the cold November weekend.

2 tablespoons unsalted butter or margarine
½ cup chopped onion
½ cup sliced celery
1 16-ounce can unsweetened solid-pack pumpkin
4 cups Turkey Frame Broth (page 146) or canned chicken broth
2 cups chopped cooked Butterball turkey
2 cups cooked wild rice
1 cup half-and-half
1 teaspoon seasoned salt
½ teaspoon ground cinnamon

Melt the butter in a large heavy saucepan over medium heat. Add the onion and celery and cook, stirring, for about 5 minutes or until softened. Add the pumpkin and broth and bring to a boil. Reduce the heat and simmer for 5 minutes.

Stir the turkey, rice, half-and-half, salt, and cinnamon into the saucepan. Heat to serving temperature but do not let boil.

CAJUN TURKEY SOUP

Serves 6

The okra and the hot pepper sauce make this soup similar to gumbo, although it is not served over rice, as gumbo generally is. Whatever you choose to call it, it is a tasty and quick soup.

2 cups chopped cooked Butterball turkey
1 clove garlic, minced
1 medium onion, sliced
2 tomatoes, chopped
1 13¾-ounce can chicken broth
1 15-ounce can tomato sauce
1 10-ounce package frozen sliced okra
¾ teaspoon hot pepper sauce
1 tablespoon sugar
½ teaspoon dried oregano
½ teaspoon salt
⅛ teaspoon dried thyme

Combine all the ingredients in a large heavy saucepan. Cook, stirring occasionally, until the vegetables are tender, about 10 minutes. Serve with additional hot pepper sauce, if desired.

SUCCOTASH TURKEY SOUP

Serves 8

As do most soups, this one tastes best made with home-made Turkey Frame Broth (page 146), but if you do not have any on hand, use canned chicken broth. The vegetable mixture and turkey pieces give the soup great flavor.

6 slices bacon
¾ cup sliced celery
½ cup thinly sliced shallots or scallions
2 large cloves garlic, minced
3 cups chopped cooked Butterball turkey
8 cups Turkey Frame Broth (page 146) or canned chicken broth
4 large tomatoes, coarsely chopped
2 cups fresh lima beans or 1 10-ounce package frozen lima beans, thawed
1½ cups whole kernel corn, fresh or frozen and thawed
¼ cup tomato paste
1½ teaspoons to 1 tablespoon chopped fresh thyme or ½ to 1 teaspoon dried
1 bay leaf
¼ teaspoon salt
¼ teaspoon coarsely ground black pepper

Cook the bacon in a heavy 4-quart saucepan over medium heat until crisp. Remove, crumble the bacon, and set aside.

Remove all but 3 tablespoons bacon drippings from the pan and reserve for another use or discard. Add the celery, shallots, and garlic to the bacon drippings remaining in the pan. Cook, stirring, for 3 to 4 minutes or until the vegetables are tender.

Add the remaining ingredients to the pan and bring to a boil over high heat. Reduce the heat to low and simmer for 30 minutes. Remove and discard the bay leaf. Serve the soup sprinkled with the crumbled bacon.

ITALIAN SAUSAGE VEGETABLE SOUP

Serves 8

This is a great way to take advantage of the robust flavor of hot turkey Italian sausage. The mixed vegetables and beans make the soup reminiscent of minestrone, and a sprinkling of grated Parmesan on top finishes it off to perfection. Mangia!

---

1 tablespoon olive oil
1 1-pound package Butterball fresh turkey Italian sausage, hot
1 large onion, chopped
3 13¾-ounce cans beef broth
1 16-ounce package frozen Italian-style vegetables
2 cups shredded green cabbage
½ teaspoon Italian seasoning
1 16-ounce can whole tomatoes, undrained and chopped
1 15-ounce can great Northern beans, drained
Grated Parmesan cheese, optional

Put the oil and the turkey sausage in a large heavy saucepan over medium-low heat. Cook, turning occasionally, for about 10 minutes or until the sausage is browned on all sides. Remove the sausage from the pan, let cool slightly, and cut the sausage into ¼-inch slices. Set the sausage aside.

Add the onion to the pan and cook for 5 minutes. Return the sliced sausage to the pan and cook with the onion until the sausage is no longer pink. Add the broth, vegetables, cabbage, and Italian seasoning. Bring the soup to a boil, reduce the heat, and simmer for 5 minutes. Add the tomatoes with their juice and the beans. Simmer for 5 minutes more. Serve sprinkled with grated Parmesan, if desired.

TURKEY BARLEY SOUP

Serves 8

Barley adds a rich, nutty flavor to turkey soup. Barley is easy to find packaged in supermarkets and is usually shelved near rice. It is also available in natural food stores.

8 cups Turkey Frame Broth (page 146) or canned
    chicken broth
½ cup chopped onion
⅓ cup uncooked medium pearl barley
1 cup diced red potato
1 cup sliced carrot
2 cups chopped cooked Butterball turkey
1 10-ounce package frozen peas
Salt
Dash of coarsely ground black pepper

Combine the broth, onion, and barley in a heavy 4-quart saucepan or stockpot. Bring to a boil over high heat. Reduce the heat to low, cover, and simmer for 30 minutes.

Add the potato and carrot to the pot and simmer for 20 minutes. Stir in the turkey and peas. Add salt and pepper to taste and simmer for 5 minutes more.

QUICK TURKEY NOODLE SOUP

Serves 6 to 8

Everyone loves turkey noodle soup and this one is fast to make and tastes grand, particularly if you use home-made broth. We have chosen frozen corn and peas, but you might prefer another vegetable, like carrots or lima beans.

8 cups Turkey Frame Broth (page 146) or canned
    chicken broth
4 ounces uncooked egg noodles
1 10-ounce package frozen whole kernel corn
1 10-ounce package frozen peas
2 cups chopped cooked Butterball turkey
Salt
Freshly ground black pepper

Bring the broth to a boil in a large heavy saucepan. Add the noodles, lower the heat, and cook according to package directions until almost tender. Add the frozen corn and peas and cook for 5 minutes more, or until the vegetables are tender. Stir in the turkey. Add salt and pepper to taste and simmer for 5 minutes more. Cook until turkey is heated through.

8

TURKEY SALADS AND SANDWICHES

We are eating more salads than ever before and easily accept them as main courses as well as side dishes. Salads appeal to us, too, because they usually include a healthful assortment of fresh vegetables or fruit and small amounts of exotic or "forbidden" ingredients, such as ripe olives, sun-dried tomatoes, and marinated artichoke hearts, providing marvelous flavors and textures. In this chapter we offer recipes for pasta salad, rice salad, potato salad, and a salad that calls for couscous. There are turkey vegetable salads, turkey fruit salads, and even a salad made with turkey sausage.

The obvious partner to salads is sandwiches. Not that the two are necessarily eaten at the same time, but both lend themselves to endless variation. Everyone loves a classic turkey sandwich on a roll with mayonnaise, lettuce, and tomato, but how about a mustard-flavored turkey salad sandwich or turkey barbecue on a bun? Our sandwiches run the gamut—some are open-faced; some are cold, others hot. All are sure to please even the most avid fan of this great culinary invention: a meal between two pieces of bread.

SWEET AND SAVORY TURKEY SALAD

Serves 6 to 8

Most people are intrigued by the flavor blend of sweet and savory ingredients. For this salad, we make a sweet and savory poppy seed dressing, relying on piquant lemon juice, vinegar, onions, and Dijon mustard to interact with the sweetness of honey and dried fruits. After an hour of sitting to give the flavors time to meld, the dressing is tossed with cold turkey, nuts, and sharp cheddar cheese.

¼ cup fresh lemon juice
¼ cup white wine vinegar
2 to 4 tablespoons Dijon mustard
2 tablespoons honey
⅔ cup vegetable oil
3 tablespoons finely chopped red onion
3 tablespoons poppy seeds
Grated zest of 1 small orange
½ cup dried apricots, cut into slivers
½ cup dried Mission figs, cut into slivers
5 cups chopped cooked Butterball turkey
4 stalks celery, coarsely chopped (about 1½ cups)
4 ounces sharp cheddar cheese, cut into 1½-inch sticks
    (about 1 cup)
¾ cup coarsely chopped pecans, lightly toasted
Green cabbage leaves
1 red cabbage or 6 to 8 red cabbage leaves

Combine the lemon juice, vinegar, mustard, and honey in a small bowl and stir until well blended. Gradually stir in the oil. Stir in the onion, poppy seeds, and orange zest. Add the apricot and fig slivers. Let the dressing stand at room temperature for 1 hour.

Put the turkey, celery, cheese, and pecans in a large bowl and toss together. Pour the poppy seed dressing over the salad and toss until well coated. Chill for several hours or overnight.

To serve, arrange the green cabbage leaves on a serving platter. Using a sharp knife, hollow out the center of the red cabbage, leaving a ½-inch shell. Spoon the salad into the hollowed-out cabbage. Or, spoon the salad onto individual red cabbage leaves. Put the filled red cabbage or filled leaves on top of the green cabbage leaves and serve.

TURKEY WALDORF SALAD

Serves 8

Here is a classic with a tasty turkey twist. Note that the mayonnaise dressing is enriched with whipped cream. Serve this salad as a main course on a bed of lettuce or in a hollowed-out red cabbage.

3 Red Delicious apples, cut into ½-inch pieces
3 Granny Smith apples, cut into ½-inch pieces
2 tablespoons fresh lemon juice
4 stalks celery, sliced
1 cup chopped pitted dates
3 cups chopped cooked Butterball turkey
½ cup mayonnaise
½ cup heavy cream, whipped
¾ cup coarsely chopped walnuts, lightly toasted
Salt
Freshly ground black pepper

Toss the apple pieces with the lemon juice in a large bowl. Add the celery, dates, and turkey and stir gently to combine.

In a separate bowl, gently fold together the mayonnaise and whipped cream. Stir the mayonnaise mixture into the salad until the ingredients are well coated. Fold in the walnuts, season with salt and pepper to taste, and serve.

GARDEN-FRESH TURKEY SALAD

Serves 4

*Yogurt and mustard form the base for this tangy dressing.
For a creamier salad, use sour cream instead of yogurt.*

¼ cup grainy Dijon mustard
¼ cup plain yogurt
2 tablespoons honey
1 tablespoon red wine vinegar
2 teaspoons poppy seeds
6 cups torn salad greens
8 cherry tomatoes, cut in half
3 cups julienne strips of cooked Butterball turkey
2 scallions, sliced on the diagonal
¼ cup sliced almonds, lightly toasted

Combine the mustard, yogurt, honey, vinegar, and
poppy seeds in a small bowl and whisk until blended.
Cover and chill for at least 1 hour.

To serve, arrange 1½ cups salad greens on each plate.
Top each with one-fourth of the tomato halves and one-
fourth of the turkey. Drizzle 3 tablespoons of the prepared dressing over each serving. Garnish with the
scallions and almonds just before serving.

TURKEY AND WILD RICE SALAD

Serves 6

Slightly crunchy, full-flavored wild rice mixed with long-grain white rice forms the base for this appetizing turkey and mushroom salad. Strips of fresh spinach leaves and bright red cherry tomatoes provide color and good flavor. Cherry tomatoes are nearly always a good choice during the off season for tomatoes. In the summer, try this salad with wedges of vine-ripened garden tomatoes.

2½ cups water
1 tablespoon unsalted butter or margarine
1 6-ounce package long grain and wild rice mix
2 cups chopped cooked Butterball turkey
¼ pound mushrooms, sliced
1 cup firmly packed spinach leaves, cut into thin strips
⅓ cup chopped fresh basil
2 scallions with tops, sliced
1 teaspoon grated lemon zest
⅓ cup dry white wine
¼ cup vegetable oil
2 teaspoons sugar
¾ teaspoon salt
¼ teaspoon freshly ground black pepper
10 cherry tomatoes, cut in half

Combine the water and butter in a medium saucepan. Stir in the rice and the contents of the seasoning packet. Bring to a boil, cover tightly, and simmer for 25 minutes or until all the water is absorbed. Transfer the rice to a large bowl, cover, and chill for 3 to 4 hours or until cold.

Add the turkey, mushrooms, spinach, basil, scallions, and lemon zest to the rice. Stir well to combine.

In a small bowl, stir together the wine, oil, sugar, salt, and pepper until blended and the sugar is dissolved. Pour the dressing over the salad and toss. Gently stir in the cherry tomatoes and serve.

SOUTHWESTERN TURKEY SALAD

Serves 4

The zippy dressing here gets its bite from horseradish and hot pepper sauce. Avocados ripen when left at room temperature and are ready for eating when they feel soft and giving.

3 cups chopped cooked Butterball turkey
½ cup sliced celery
½ cup chopped red bell pepper
2 tablespoons chopped scallions
1 8-ounce jar taco sauce
½ cup chili sauce
1 tablespoon fresh lime juice
1 tablespoon prepared horseradish
¼ teaspoon hot pepper sauce
1 avocado, peeled, pitted, and cut into pieces
6 cups torn salad greens
Chopped fresh cilantro, optional

Put the turkey, celery, bell pepper, and scallions in a large bowl. Combine the taco sauce, chili sauce, lime juice, horseradish, and hot pepper sauce in a small bowl. Pour over the turkey and vegetables and toss to mix. Cover and chill for several hours.

Just before serving, gently stir the avocado into the turkey mixture. Arrange the salad greens on a serving platter and top with the turkey salad. Sprinkle with the cilantro, if desired, and serve.

FRENCH TURKEY POTATO SALAD

Serves 4

Sour cream, Dijon mustard, herbs, and spices combine to make a dressing that is served cold, but has discernible "heat" to it. Mild-tasting turkey and red potatoes blend well with this creation.

3 tablespoons Dijon mustard
¾ cup sour cream
½ teaspoon ground coriander
¼ teaspoon ground ginger
¼ teaspoon ground cumin
½ teaspoon hot pepper sauce
2½ cups chopped cooked Butterball turkey
6 small red potatoes, unpeeled, cooked, and diced
    (2 cups)
½ cup cooked peas
¾ cup sliced celery
1 medium onion, chopped
Salt

Put the mustard, sour cream, coriander, ginger, cumin, and hot pepper sauce in a small bowl and stir until well combined.

Put the turkey, potatoes, peas, celery, and onion in a medium bowl. Season with salt to taste. Spoon the dressing over the turkey mixture and stir gently until the ingredients are evenly coated. Cover and refrigerate for several hours. Serve chilled.

CURRIED COUSCOUS AND TURKEY SALAD

Serves 6 to 8

Couscous is sold in supermarkets, Middle Eastern markets, natural food stores, and many specialty markets. Made from precooked semolina or whole-wheat flour, it cooks quickly and, for cooking purposes, is considered a grain.

1 cup chicken broth
½ teaspoon salt
½ teaspoon curry powder
1 cup couscous
½ cup golden raisins
2 tablespoons finely chopped crystallized ginger
1 cup mayonnaise
3 tablespoons fresh lemon juice
3 cups chopped cooked Butterball turkey
⅓ cup chopped celery
⅓ cup thinly sliced scallions
⅓ cup slivered almonds, lightly toasted
1 cup seedless red grapes, cut in half
1 orange, peeled and white pith removed, cut into pieces
3 tablespoons chopped parsley

Bring the broth, salt, and curry powder to a boil in a medium saucepan over high heat. Stir in the couscous, raisins, and ginger. Remove from the heat, cover, and let stand for 5 minutes. Fluff up the couscous with a fork and let cool to room temperature.

Combine the mayonnaise with the lemon juice in a large bowl and stir to mix. Add the turkey, celery, scallions, almonds, and couscous mixture. Stir together gently. Fold in the grapes, orange pieces, and parsley. Cover and refrigerate for several hours.

TURKEY AND ORANGE SALAD WITH POPPY SEED DRESSING

Serves 4

Poppy seeds and citrus fruit are particularly well suited to each other. And the light flavor of turkey makes it a perfect match with sliced oranges.

4 tablespoons fresh lemon juice
2 tablespoons vegetable oil
2 teaspoons sugar
½ teaspoon poppy seeds
½ teaspoon soy sauce
Lettuce leaves
8 slices cooked Butterball turkey
4 oranges, peeled and white pith removed, sliced
    crosswise

Put the lemon juice, oil, sugar, poppy seeds, and soy sauce in a container with a tight-fitting lid and shake to combine. Let the dressing stand for 30 minutes.

Arrange lettuce leaves on 4 serving plates. Top with the turkey and orange slices and spoon dressing over the top.

TARRAGON TURKEY PASTA SALAD

Serves 6 to 8

Pasta salads are great favorites on warm summer evenings. Quick to prepare, this one is made with frozen vegetables and bottled salad dressing. Depending on your family's preference, choose a mild or tangy dressing, but keep in mind that garlic and tarragon are added to it to perk it up.

1 cup creamy dressing, such as ranch or creamy Italian
1 clove garlic, minced
1 tablespoon dried tarragon, crushed
2 cups chopped cooked Butterball turkey
4 cups cooked rotini pasta (2½ cups uncooked)
2 cups frozen mixed Italian-style vegetables, thawed and drained
1 small red onion, thinly sliced
Salt
Freshly ground black pepper

Blend the creamy dressing with the garlic and tarragon. Put the turkey, cooked pasta, and vegetables in a large bowl. Add the dressing and toss the salad until well coated. Season with salt and pepper to taste.

TURKEY PAPAYA SALAD

Serves 4

This salad is meant to be served slightly warm or at room temperature—not chilled. If you have not had papaya, one taste of this tropical fruit will lead you to understand why much of the world's population is sold on it. Ripe papaya is yellow colored and feels soft and gives to the touch, similar to ripe avocado.

1 papaya or small cantaloupe, peeled, seeded, and cut into 1½ × ¾-inch pieces
1 medium sweet onion, slivered
2 tablespoons chopped chives
1 tablespoon fresh lemon juice
1 tablespoon Dijon mustard
¼ teaspoon salt
⅛ teaspoon freshly ground black pepper
⅓ cup olive oil
1 1-pound package Butterball fresh boneless turkey breast strips
Lettuce or spinach leaves

Put the papaya, onion, and chives in a large bowl and set aside. In a small bowl, stir together the lemon juice, mustard, salt, and pepper.

Heat the oil in a large skillet over medium heat. Add the turkey strips and cook, stirring occasionally, for about 4 minutes or until no longer pink. Remove the turkey from the pan with a slotted spoon and add to the papaya mixture.

Let the oil in the skillet cool slightly. Add the mustard mixture and whisk to blend. Pour the dressing over the turkey papaya mixture. Toss together and serve at once on lettuce leaves.

ITALIAN TURKEY SAUSAGE AND TORTELLINI SALAD

Serves 6

The sunny flavors of the Mediterranean joyfully compete with one another in this robust tortellini salad. Cheese-filled tortellini is found in the refrigerator or frozen food sections of the supermarket or may be bought at specialty stores selling fresh pasta.

1 1-pound package Butterball fresh turkey Italian sausage, mild
5 tablespoons vegetable oil, divided
1 9-ounce package fresh cheese-filled tortellini
1 6½-ounce jar marinated artichoke hearts, drained, marinade reserved
½ cup sliced pitted ripe olives
½ cup crumbled feta cheese
¼ cup sliced scallions
6 sun-dried tomatoes, packed in oil, drained, and cut into strips (about ¼ cup)
2 tablespoons white wine vinegar
1 clove garlic, minced
1 teaspoon dried basil
¼ teaspoon dried dillweed
½ cup torn fresh spinach leaves

Put the turkey sausage in a large skillet with 1 tablespoon of the oil. Cook over medium-low heat for 8 to 10 minutes, turning occasionally, until browned on all sides. Reduce the heat to low, cover, and continue to cook for 8 to 10 minutes more, turning once. Alternatively, the sausage may be grilled or broiled 4 inches from the heat for about 8 minutes on each side. Let the sausage cool and cut into ¼-inch slices.

Cook the tortellini according to package directions. Drain, rinse, drain again well, and toss with 1 tablespoon of the oil.

Combine the tortellini, sliced sausage, artichoke hearts, olives, feta cheese, scallions, and tomato strips in a large bowl. Put the reserved artichoke marinade (about ¼ cup) in a small bowl. Add the remaining 3 tablespoons oil, vinegar, garlic, basil, and dill weed and whisk to combine.

Pour the dressing over the sausage-tortellini mixture. Cover and refrigerate for several hours.

To serve, stir in the spinach and let the salad stand at room temperature for 30 minutes before serving.

TURKEY PITA PIZZAS

Serves 8

2 cups chopped cooked Butterball turkey
1 14-ounce jar pizza sauce
5 fully cooked sausage links, cut crosswise into slices
1 2-ounce can sliced mushrooms, drained
½ cup chopped green bell pepper
½ cup sliced pitted ripe olives
8 pita pockets
2 cups (8 ounces) shredded mozzarella cheese
¼ cup grated Parmesan cheese

Preheat the oven to 400°F.

Combine the turkey, pizza sauce, sausage slices, mushrooms, bell pepper, and olives in a bowl. Spread ½ cup of this mixture onto each pita bread. Put the pitas on a baking sheet and sprinkle with the cheeses. Bake for 10 to 12 minutes or until the sandwiches are hot and the cheese is melted.

HOT TURKEY HERO

Serves 4

Made with dark rye, this "hero" is served warm, with plenty of melted cheese and thick turkey slices.

4 tablespoons unsalted butter or margarine
1½ cups sliced onion
1½ cups sliced green bell pepper
⅓ cup white wine vinegar
8 slices cooked Butterball turkey
8 slices dark rye bread
Horseradish sauce or Dijon mustard
12 thin slices salami
8 slices aged Swiss or provolone cheese (4 ounces)

Preheat the broiler.

Melt 2 tablespoons of the butter in a skillet over medium heat. Add the onion and pepper and cook, stirring occasionally, until softened. Stir in the vinegar. Remove the onion mixture from the skillet and keep warm.

Melt the remaining 2 tablespoons butter in the same skillet. Add the turkey and warm, turning, until heated through and lightly browned.

Toast the bread slices on one side only under the broiler. Lightly spread the untoasted side with horseradish sauce. Divide the turkey among 4 slices of the bread. Top with salami. Spoon the onion mixture over the salami and cover with cheese. Broil until the cheese is melted. Top with the remaining 4 slices of bread and serve immediately.

TURKEY BARBECUE ON BUNS

Serves 8

2 tablespoons unsalted butter or margarine
½ cup chopped celery
¼ cup chopped onion
¼ cup chopped green bell pepper
2 cups chopped cooked Butterball turkey
1 cup ketchup
3 tablespoons vinegar
2 tablespoons brown sugar
½ teaspoon dry mustard
¼ teaspoon salt
8 hamburger buns, split and toasted

Melt the butter in a skillet over medium heat. Add the celery, onion, and bell pepper and cook until lightly browned. Add the turkey, ketchup, vinegar, brown sugar, mustard, and salt. Reduce the heat to low and simmer for 10 to 15 minutes.

Spoon the turkey barbecue on the bottom halves of the buns. Cover with the top halves and serve.

9

TURKEY SAUSAGES

Seasoned with mild herbs or fiery spices, turkey sausages are a welcome change from pork sausages. They are lower in fat and calories but score just as high when it comes to flavor. Butterball turkey sausages blend magically with other ingredients to make terrific suppers, lunch dishes, and, of course, breakfast fare. Whether you break apart the sausage meat during cooking or leave it in its link shape, make sure it is cooked through and no longer pink.

SMOKED SAUSAGE NOODLE BAKE

Serves 4 to 6

In this one-dish meal, smoked sausage pieces are nestled on a bed of creamy noodles.

6 ounces uncooked medium-width egg noodles
2 tablespoons unsalted butter or margarine
½ cup chopped onion
½ cup chopped celery
1 17-ounce can cream-style corn
½ cup sour cream
½ teaspoon salt
Dash of freshly ground black pepper
1 1-pound package Butterball turkey smoked sausage

Preheat the oven to 350°F. Butter an 11 × 7 × 2-inch baking dish. Cook the noodles according to package directions. Do not overcook them. Drain and set aside.

Meanwhile, melt the butter in a small saucepan over medium heat. Add the onion and celery and cook, stirring occasionally, until softened.

Combine the noodles with the onion-celery mixture, corn, sour cream, salt, and pepper. Pour into the prepared baking dish. Cut the sausage into serving-sized pieces. Put the sausage pieces on top of the noodles, pushing the sausage partially down into the noodles. Bake for 40 minutes or until hot.

VERMONT VEGETABLE STEW

Serves 8

This one-dish meal cooks in 45 minutes.

1 tablespoon vegetable oil
1 medium onion, chopped
1 1-pound package Butterball turkey smoked sausage, thinly sliced
3 cups water
2 teaspoons beef bouillon granules
1 bay leaf
½ teaspoon dried thyme
3 carrots, sliced
3 stalks celery, sliced
¼ head green cabbage, cut into chunks
2 tablespoons uncooked rice
1 8-ounce can tomato sauce
1 15-ounce can red kidney beans
1 28-ounce can whole tomatoes, undrained and cut up

Heat the oil in a large deep saucepan over medium heat. Add the onion and cook, stirring occasionally, until softened. Add the remaining ingredients and bring to a boil over high heat. Lower the heat, cover, and simmer for 30 minutes or until the vegetables are tender.

SMOKED SAUSAGE AND SWEET POTATO SKILLET SUPPER

Serves 4 to 5

Sweet potatoes in syrup and a firm, ripe pear are a great match for smoked sausage. Bartlett and Anjou pears are good choices for this dish. Try to buy unblemished fruit and use it before it feels too soft. A firm pear will hold its shape during cooking.

1 1-pound package Butterball turkey smoked sausage
1 16-ounce can cut sweet potatoes in light syrup
1 large firm green pear, cored and cut into pieces

Cut the sausage into serving-sized pieces. Put the sausage pieces, undrained sweet potatoes, and pear in a large skillet. Bring the syrup to a boil, cover, and simmer for 9 to 10 minutes or until the sausage is hot. If a thicker sauce is desired, uncover and continue to cook until the liquid is reduced to the desired consistency.

PIZZA FRANKS

Serves 8 or makes 40 appetizers

Turkey franks are just right for splitting and filling with a yummy mixture of pizza sauce, vegetables, and cheese.

1 tablespoon unsalted butter or margarine
¼ cup finely chopped onion
¼ cup finely chopped green bell pepper
¼ cup finely chopped mushrooms
1 1-pound package Butterball turkey franks
3 tablespoons pizza sauce
½ cup (2 ounces) shredded mozzarella cheese
Hot dog buns, optional

Preheat the oven to 350°F.

Melt the butter in a medium skillet over medium heat. Add the onion, bell pepper, and mushrooms and cook, stirring, for about 3 minutes or until crisp-tender.

Make a lengthwise slit in each frank, being careful not to cut through to the underside. Spread about 1 teaspoon pizza sauce in each opened frank. Sprinkle each with a little of the mozzarella, reserving about ¼ cup for the top. Add the vegetable mixture, dividing it evenly among the franks.

Put the filled franks in an 11 × 7-inch baking dish and sprinkle with the remaining cheese. Bake, uncovered, for 15 to 20 minutes. Serve in buns, if desired. Or, cut each frank into 5 pieces and serve as an appetizer.

SAUSAGE-PEPPER-PASTA TOSS

Serves 6

*Sausages and peppers are a marriage made in culinary
heaven. When the sausage is a turkey sausage, the union
is guaranteed bliss. In this recipe we have included eggplant and lots of good seasonings to make this pasta toss
one of the best ever.*

1 medium eggplant, cut into ½-inch slices
4 to 5 tablespoons olive oil
8 ounces uncooked rotini pasta
1 1-pound package Butterball fresh turkey Italian
    sausage, hot
2 medium red bell peppers, cut into ¼-inch strips
1 large onion, chopped
2 cloves garlic, minced
1 cup half-and-half
1 teaspoon chicken bouillon granules
½ teaspoon Italian seasoning
⅓ cup chopped parsley
¼ cup grated Parmesan cheese plus more for sprinkling

Preheat the broiler.

Brush the eggplant slices with oil and put them on a
baking sheet. Broil 4 inches from the heat for about 7
minutes on each side or until golden brown. Set aside.
When the eggplant slices are cool, cut them into ½-inch
strips.

Cook the rotini in boiling water in a large heavy saucepan according to package directions. Rinse and drain well. Return to the pan, toss with 1 tablespoon olive oil, cover, and set aside.

Put 1 tablespoon olive oil and the turkey sausage in a large skillet. Cook for 8 to 10 minutes over medium-low heat, turning occasionally. Reduce the heat to low, cover, and continue to cook for 8 to 10 minutes more, turning once. Remove the sausage from the pan and set aside to cool slightly. Cut the sausage into ¼-inch slices.

Add the bell peppers, onion, and garlic to the skillet. Cook for 5 minutes over medium heat, stirring occasionally. Add the half-and-half, bouillon granules, and Italian seasoning and bring to a boil. Stir in the parsley and the ¼ cup Parmesan cheese.

Pour the sauce over the pasta. Add the reserved sausage and eggplant and toss gently. Cover and heat through gently for 2 to 3 minutes or until hot. Serve with additional Parmesan cheese.

TURKEY SAUSAGE POT PIE

Serves 4

This is a pot pie with a difference: The topping is fashioned from cornbread sticks rather than the expected pie crust. Beneath the cornbread are layers of sausages and vegetables and meltingly good ricotta and mozzarella cheeses.

1 tablespoon olive oil
1 1-pound package Butterball fresh turkey Italian sausage, mild
1 15-ounce can pizza sauce
1 10-ounce package frozen Italian-style vegetables with sauce
1 cup ricotta cheese
2 tablespoons grated Parmesan cheese
¼ teaspoon Italian seasoning
2 cups (8 ounces) shredded mozzarella cheese
1 7-ounce package refrigerated cornbread stick dough
Italian seasoning, optional
Grated Parmesan cheese, optional

Preheat the oven to 375°F. Butter an 11 × 7-inch baking dish.

Combine the oil and sausage in a large skillet. Cook over medium heat for 8 to 10 minutes or until browned. Cool slightly and cut into ¼-inch slices. Return the sausage to the skillet, add the pizza sauce, and bring to a boil. Reduce the heat to low, cover, and simmer for 5 minutes. Add the vegetables, cover, and simmer for 5 minutes more.

Meanwhile, stir together the ricotta, Parmesan, and Italian seasoning in a medium bowl.

To assemble, spread half the sausage mixture in the prepared baking dish. Dot with half the ricotta-Parmesan mixture and sprinkle with half the mozzarella. Repeat the layers.

Cover the dish with aluminum foil and bake for 20 minutes. Remove the foil and place twisted cornbread dough across the top of the casserole. If desired, sprinkle with additional Italian seasoning and/or Parmesan cheese. Bake for 12 minutes or until the cornbread sticks are golden brown.

TURKEY BREAKFAST SAUSAGE BURRITO

Serves 1

For more than one serving, repeat this procedure as many times over as necessary. To warm the flour tortilla, which is larger and milder tasting than a corn tortilla, wrap it in foil and set it in a warm (300°F.) oven or toaster oven for two to three minutes. Or, put it on a microwave-safe plate and microwave it on High (100 percent) power for 10 seconds or until warm.

1 large egg
1 teaspoon water
1 teaspoon unsalted butter or margarine
2 teaspoons sliced scallion
1 flour tortilla, warmed
2 hot cooked Butterball fresh turkey breakfast sausage
    links
Shredded Monterey Jack or cheddar cheese
Salsa or chili sauce

Beat the egg with the water in a small bowl and set aside. Melt the butter in a small skillet over medium heat. Add the scallion and cook for about 30 seconds. Add the egg, stirring to scramble.

To assemble, put the tortilla on a plate. Spread the scrambled egg down the center of the upper half of the tortilla. Add the turkey sausage links, sprinkle with the cheese, and top with salsa. Fold up the lower half of the tortilla and fold in the sides.

TURKEY BREAKFAST SAUSAGE WITH FRUIT COMPOTE

Serves 5 to 6

Sausages cooked with a sweet compote of dried and canned fruit make an unexpected and satisfying topping for waffles or French toast.

1 6-ounce package dried apricots
1 6-ounce can unsweetened pineapple juice
2 teaspoons vegetable oil
1 14-ounce package Butterball fresh turkey breakfast sausage links
1 8¼-ounce can sweetened pineapple chunks, undrained
1 tablespoon honey
Dash of grated nutmeg
½ cup seedless green grapes
Hot waffles or French toast

Combine the apricots and pineapple juice in a medium saucepan and bring to a boil over medium heat. Cover, reduce the heat, and simmer for 10 minutes.

Meanwhile, put the oil and breakfast sausage in a large skillet. Cook over medium heat for about 7 minutes, turning to brown evenly.

Add the undrained pineapple, honey, and nutmeg to the apricots and stir. Pour the fruit mixture over the sausage and simmer for 5 minutes. Stir in the grapes.

Serve over waffles or French toast.

10

STUFFINGS AND DRESSINGS

For some people, the best part of a turkey dinner is the stuffing. Whether the savory mixture is actually stuffed into the turkey's cavities (stuffing) or served on the side as a casserole (dressing), it is integral to many a turkey feast. Here we have thoroughly modern stuffings and dressings as well as a smattering of old-fashioned formulas of which we never seem to tire.

Stuffings and dressings should be made shortly before cooking. For plan-ahead cooking, chop and measure the ingredients in advance, keeping the dry and moist ones separate until it is time to combine them for the recipe. If you use any of these stuffing recipes, roast the bird immediately after stuffing it. For safety reasons, never hold a dressed uncooked turkey in the refrigerator or at room temperature. After the meal, remove the stuffing from the turkey cavities and refrigerate the leftover turkey and stuffing separately.

CONFETTI CORNBREAD STUFFING

*Makes about 16 cups;
enough for a 20- to 24-pound turkey*

The colorful vegetables in this stuffing resemble party confetti—and surely this tasty mixture is the right choice for a big gathering. Kale is sold in green grocers and many supermarkets, and fennel, which looks rather like a bulbous head of celery with feathery greens, is easy to find, too. It tastes like licorice, and you will detect that flavor among the others here.

---

1 pound kale, center ribs removed and torn into
    1-inch pieces
16 tablespoons (2 sticks) unsalted butter or margarine
2 medium red bell peppers, chopped
1 large onion, chopped
1 medium bulb fennel, coarsely chopped
4 cloves garlic, minced
3 8-ounce packages cornbread stuffing crumbs
2 pounds hot-and-spicy smoked Polish sausage, cut on
    the diagonal into ¼-inch slices
1 14-ounce can cream-style corn
1½ cups (6 ounces) shredded sharp cheddar cheese
½ cup pine nuts, lightly toasted
2½ cups chicken broth
1 tablespoon dried oregano, crushed
Salt
Freshly ground black pepper

Bring a large saucepan of water to a boil. Add the kale and cook for 5 minutes or until just tender. Drain in a colander. Cool slightly and, using your hands, squeeze out excess moisture. Set aside.

Heat 12 tablespoons (1½ sticks) of the butter in a large skillet over medium-high heat until melted. Add the bell peppers, onion, fennel, and garlic. Cook, stirring frequently, for 10 minutes or until the vegetables are softened. Transfer the mixture to a large bowl, add the stuffing crumbs, and cooked kale, and toss to mix.

In the same skillet, cook the sausage in small batches, stirring frequently, until browned all over. Add the sausage to the stuffing in the bowl along with any accumulated pan drippings. Stir in the corn, cheese, and pine nuts until well combined.

Combine the chicken broth with the remaining 4 tablespoons butter in a medium saucepan. Cook, stirring, over medium-high heat until the butter is melted. Pour over the stuffing to moisten and toss gently to mix. Stir in the oregano and salt and pepper to taste.

Put the stuffing in the neck and body cavities of a 20- to 24-pound Butterball turkey. Put any remaining stuffing in a buttered casserole and bake, covered, with the turkey during the last 40 minutes of roasting.

MUSHROOM SAGE STUFFING

*Makes about 10 cups;
enough for a 14- to 16-pound turkey*

This is a classic onion and sage stuffing enriched with rye bread, mushrooms, and chestnuts. To peel chestnuts, cut a slit on the flat side of the hard brown shell. Put the chestnuts in boiling water, and simmer them for about 2 to 3 minutes. Drain, and while still warm, use a sharp knife to peel the shell and skin from the nutmeat. If the skins are difficult to remove, drop into boiling water for a few seconds.

8 cups rye bread cubes (10 to 12 slices bread, cubed)
8 tablespoons (1 stick) unsalted butter or margarine
1 large onion, finely chopped
2 cloves garlic, minced
4 stalks celery, chopped
1 pound mushrooms, trimmed and sliced
½ cup cream sherry
1½ pounds chestnuts, peeled and coarsely chopped
2 teaspoons rubbed sage
1 teaspoon dried thyme
1 bunch parsley, finely chopped
Salt
Freshly ground black pepper
½ cup Giblet Broth (page 257) or chicken broth, if
    needed

Preheat the oven to 300°F.

Spread the cubed bread on a large baking sheet and toast in the oven for about 15 minutes or until lightly browned. Cool and transfer to a large bowl. Raise the oven temperature to 325°F.

Melt the butter in a large skillet over medium heat. Add the onion, garlic, and celery and cook for 10 minutes, stirring occasionally. Stir in the mushrooms and sherry and continue to cook for 10 minutes more, stirring frequently.

Add the vegetables, including liquid, to the cubed bread and mix well. Add the chestnuts, sage, thyme, and parsley. Season with salt and pepper to taste. If the stuffing seems a little dry, moisten with giblet stock or chicken broth.

Put the stuffing in the neck and body cavities of a 14- to 16-pound Butterball turkey. Put any remaining stuffing in a buttered casserole and bake, covered, with the turkey during the last 40 minutes of roasting.

CORNBREAD, SAUSAGE, AND CRANBERRY STUFFING

Makes about 10 cups;
enough for a 14- to 16-pound turkey

Use your favorite recipe for cornbread for this stuffing, or make cornbread from a seven and a half-ounce package of corn muffin mix. To chop the cranberries, process them briefly in the food processor or blender. Do not overchop them.

---

1 pound sweet Italian sausage, bulk, or links, casings
    removed
6 tablespoons unsalted butter or margarine
1 large onion, chopped
4 stalks celery, chopped
2 carrots, coarsely grated
6 cups day-old cornbread, crumbled
2 cups cranberries, coarsely chopped
3 tablespoons maple syrup
Finely grated zest of 1 orange
3 tablespoons fresh rosemary, coarsely chopped,
    or 1 tablespoon dried
Salt
Freshly ground black pepper

Cook the sausage in a large skillet over medium-high heat for 10 to 15 minutes until the meat is browned. Use a wooden spoon to break up the sausage. Remove from the skillet with a slotted spoon and put in a large bowl.

Add the butter to the sausage drippings in the skillet and melt over medium heat. Add the onion, celery, and carrots and cook for about 15 minutes or until the vegetables are softened. Add the vegetables to the sausage in the bowl. Stir in the cornbread.

Combine the chopped cranberries with the maple syrup and add to the stuffing in the bowl. Stir in the orange zest and rosemary. Season with salt and pepper to taste.

Put the stuffing in the neck and body cavities of a 14- to 16-pound Butterball turkey. Put any remaining stuffing in a buttered casserole and bake, covered, with the turkey during the last 45 to 60 minutes of roasting.

CORNBREAD-PECAN STUFFING

Makes 8 cups;
enough for a 12-pound turkey

Use your own recipe for cornbread or a seven and a half-ounce package of corn muffin mix. To toast the pecans, spread them in a single layer in a shallow pan and put them in a moderate (350°F.) oven for about 5 to 10 minutes. Shake the pan a few times, and when they smell fragrant and have darkened a little, transfer them to another pan or plate to cool. Toasting nuts brings out their best flavor.

5 cups fresh bread cubes, crusts removed (about 8
    slices fresh bread)
5 cups crumbled cornbread
8 tablespoons (1 stick) unsalted butter or margarine
1 cup chopped onion
½ cup chopped green bell pepper
½ cup chopped red bell pepper
¾ teaspoon poultry seasoning
¼ teaspoon salt
¼ teaspoon grated nutmeg
⅛ teaspoon freshly ground black pepper
½ cup coarsely chopped pecans, lightly toasted
½ to ¾ cup Giblet Broth (page 257) or chicken broth
1 large egg, beaten

Combine the bread cubes and cornbread in a large bowl. Melt the butter in a medium skillet over medium heat. Add the onion and bell peppers and cook until softened. Stir in the poultry seasoning, salt, nutmeg, and black pepper.

Add the vegetable mixture, pecans, stock, and egg to the bread mixture and toss to combine. Put the stuffing in the neck and body cavities of a 12-pound Butterball turkey. Put any remaining stuffing in a buttered casserole, cover, and bake with the turkey during the last 30 to 45 minutes of roasting.

BROWN 'N SERVE SAUSAGE STUFFING

Makes about 8 cups;
enough for a 12- to 14-pound turkey

1 8-ounce package Brown 'N Serve sausage links,
   original variety
4 tablespoons unsalted butter or margarine
1 cup chopped celery
1 cup chopped onion
1 16-ounce package herb-seasoned stuffing cubes
2 teaspoons rubbed sage
2 cups chicken broth

Cut the sausage into pieces. Melt the butter in a medium skillet over medium heat. Add the sausage, celery, and onion and cook, stirring occasionally, until the sausage is browned and the vegetables are softened.

Combine the stuffing cubes, sausage mixture, and sage in a large bowl. Add the broth and stir gently until evenly moistened.

Put the stuffing in the neck and body cavities of a 12- to 14-pound Butterball turkey. Put any remaining stuffing in a buttered casserole and bake, covered, with the turkey during the last 45 minutes of roasting.

DRIED FRUIT AND
APPLE CIDER BREAD DRESSING

Makes about 6 cups;
not recommended as a stuffing

Use the tastiest apple cider you can buy. The best usually comes from local orchards that make it during apple season. Because it is not pasteurized, apple cider does not keep as long as bottled apple juice.

4 tablespoons unsalted butter or margarine
1 cup chopped celery
½ cup chopped onion
1 7-ounce package herb-seasoned stuffing cubes
1 6-ounce package diced dried mixed fruit
½ cup chopped walnuts
1½ cups apple cider
1 tablespoon packed brown sugar
½ teaspoon ground cinnamon

Preheat the oven to 325°F. Butter a 1½-quart casserole.
Melt the butter in a medium skillet over medium heat. Add the celery and onion and cook until crisp-tender. Remove from the heat.
Put the remaining ingredients in a large bowl. Add the celery-onion mixture and stir to mix.
Put the dressing in the prepared casserole, cover, and bake for 50 minutes.

OLD-FASHIONED BREAD STUFFING

Makes about 8 cups;
enough for a 12- to 14-pound turkey

Regardless of how far afield we go searching for new and innovative ways to make turkey stuffing, some things cannot be improved upon. This old-time bread stuffing is one of the classics.

8 tablespoons (1 stick) unsalted butter or margarine
1½ cups chopped onion
1½ cups chopped celery
1 teaspoon poultry seasoning
1 teaspoon rubbed sage
1 teaspoon salt
Dash of freshly ground black pepper
8 cups slightly dried white or whole-wheat bread cubes
     (10 to 12 bread slices, cubed and dried overnight)
½ cup water or chicken broth

Melt the butter in a medium skillet over medium heat. Add the onion and celery and cook, stirring occasionally, until softened. Stir in the seasonings.

Put the bread cubes in a large bowl. Add the onion mixture and water and toss to mix.

Put the stuffing in the neck and body cavities of a 12- to 14-pound Butterball turkey. Put any remaining stuffing in a buttered casserole and bake, covered, with the turkey during the last 45 minutes of roasting.

Bacon and Green Pepper stuffing: Substitute 1½ cups chopped green bell pepper for the celery. Substitute 1 teaspoon dried thyme for the poultry seasoning and sage. Reduce salt to ½ teaspoon. Add 12 slices diced cooked bacon to the bread cubes.

APPLE WILD RICE DRESSING

Makes about 8 cups;
not recommended as a stuffing

⅔ cup wild rice, rinsed and drained
2 tablespoons chicken bouillon granules
3 cups water
½ cup uncooked long-grain rice
⅓ cup unsalted butter or margarine
½ cup chopped celery
⅓ cup chopped onion
1 cup chopped apple
1½ cups slightly dried white or whole-wheat bread
    cubes (2 to 2½ slices bread, cubed and dried
    overnight)
½ cup chopped pecans, toasted
½ cup raisins
1 large egg, beaten
1 teaspoon poultry seasoning
¼ teaspoon rubbed sage

Preheat the oven to 325°F. Butter a 2-quart casserole.
   Combine the wild rice, bouillon granules, and water in a medium saucepan and bring to a boil over high heat. Reduce the heat, cover, and simmer for 20 minutes. Add the long-grain rice, cover, and simmer 25 minutes more or until the water is absorbed.

Meanwhile, melt the butter in a medium skillet over medium heat. Add the celery and onion and cook until softened. Combine the rice and the celery mixture in a large bowl. The dressing can be made up to this point the night before. Keep it covered in the refrigerator until 1 hour before completing the recipe to allow it time to come to room temperature.

Add the remaining ingredients and stir until well mixed. Put the dressing in the prepared casserole, cover, and bake for 35 minutes. Remove the cover and bake for 15 minutes more or until hot.

BELL PEPPER AND CILANTRO DRESSING

Makes about 8 cups;
not recommended as a stuffing

This spirited dressing reflects the sunny flavors of the Southwest. Rather than bolster the dressing with a meat such as sausage, which is quite common, this recipe uses smoked turkey breast. Cilantro, also called Chinese parsley and coriander, is a dark green herb sold in many greengrocers and supermarkets.

4 tablespoons unsalted butter or margarine
2 tablespoons vegetable oil
1½ cups chopped onion
1½ cups chopped red bell pepper
1½ cups chopped green bell pepper
2 jalapeño peppers, seeded and finely chopped
½ teaspoon salt
¼ teaspoon ground cumin
⅛ teaspoon freshly ground black pepper
1 7-ounce package unseasoned dried bread cubes
1 cup frozen whole kernel corn, thawed
1 6-ounce package Butterball smoked turkey breast slices, cut into julienne strips
⅓ cup chopped fresh cilantro
¼ cup sliced scallions
1 cup chicken broth

Preheat the oven to 325°F. Butter a 2-quart casserole.

Melt the butter with the oil in a medium skillet over medium heat. Add the onion, bell peppers, and jalapeño peppers and cook, stirring, for 12 to 15 minutes. Stir in the salt, cumin, and black pepper.

In a large bowl, combine the bread cubes, corn, smoked turkey, cilantro, and scallions. Add the pepper mixture and broth and toss gently until combined.

Put the dressing in the prepared casserole, cover, and bake for 45 minutes or until hot.

WILD RICE, SAUSAGE, AND OYSTER DRESSING

*Makes about 14 cups;
not recommended as a stuffing*

This would be a good choice for Christmas or New Year's Eve when you want to make a very special, festive dressing. Oysters are traditional during the holidays, and wild rice, which actually is the seed of a grasslike plant, is a luxury whose nutty flavor makes it well worth the extravagance. Buy the oysters from a reputable fish merchant and, if possible, ask him to shuck them in front of you to ensure their freshness. Wild rice is sold in specialty shops, natural food stores, and many supermarkets.

⅔ cup wild rice, rinsed and drained
1 pint shucked fresh oysters
1 pound bulk pork sausage, or links, casings removed
8 tablespoons (1 stick) unsalted butter or margarine
2 cups chopped celery
3 medium carrots, coarsely grated
1 large onion, chopped (about 1 cup)
¾ pound mushrooms, sliced (about 4½ cups)
⅓ cup brandy, optional
1 8-ounce package cornbread stuffing crumbs
1 cup hazelnuts, lightly toasted, skinned, and coarsely chopped
1 large egg, beaten
Salt
Freshly ground black pepper

Preheat the oven to 350°F. Butter a shallow 3-quart casserole.

Cook the wild rice according to package directions. Drain the rice and put it in a large bowl. Drain the oysters, reserving ½ cup of their liquor. Coarsely chop the oysters and add them to the wild rice in the bowl.

In a large skillet, cook the sausage over medium-high heat until browned, stirring occasionally to break up the meat. Drain thoroughly and add to the rice mixture.

Using the same skillet, melt the butter over medium-high heat. Add the celery, carrots, and onion and cook, stirring, for 5 to 7 minutes or until the vegetables are crisp-tender. Stir in the mushrooms, brandy, if using, and the reserved oyster liquor. Cook, stirring, for 10 minutes or until the liquid has evaporated.

Add the vegetables to the rice mixture, stirring until well combined. Stir in the cornbread stuffing crumbs and hazelnuts, tossing lightly until well mixed. Stir in the beaten egg until blended. Season with salt and pepper to taste.

Put the dressing in the prepared casserole and bake, uncovered, for 40 to 50 minutes.

RICE PRIMAVERA DRESSING

Makes about 8 cups;
not recommended as a stuffing

*Rice is a welcome change from bread as the base for
dressing. We suggest cooking the rice for this recipe in
chicken broth to give it extra flavor. Regular long-grain
rather than "minute" rice is recommended.*

2 teaspoons unsalted butter or margarine
1 cup chopped celery
1 cup sliced leeks
1 cup asparagus pieces
6 cups hot long-grain rice, cooked in chicken broth
½ cup slivered almonds, lightly toasted
1 teaspoon grated lemon zest
¼ teaspoon salt
Dash of freshly ground black pepper

Preheat the oven to 325°F. Butter a 2- to 2½-quart casserole.

Melt the butter in a large skillet over medium heat.
Add the celery and cook, stirring, for 2 to 3 minutes
until slightly softened. Add the leeks and asparagus,
cover, and cook over medium-low heat for 4 to 5 minutes.

Put the rice, almonds, lemon zest, salt, and pepper in
a large bowl. Add the vegetable mixture and stir to mix.
Put the dressing in the prepared casserole, cover, and
bake for 35 minutes or until hot.

PROSCIUTTO AND BARLEY DRESSING

Makes about 8 cups

The combination of prosciutto and barley is one you do not expect to find with turkey, but the flavors work wonderfully together. Barley is sold in many supermarkets and also in natural food stores. Follow the package directions for cooking it.

8 tablespoons (1 stick) unsalted butter or margarine
1½ cups chopped onion
1½ cups chopped celery
2 teaspoons dried thyme
4 ounces thinly sliced prosciutto or Canadian bacon, cut into julienne strips
1 7-ounce package herb-seasoned stuffing cubes
2 cups cooked barley
1 cup chicken broth

Preheat the oven to 350°F. Butter a 2-quart casserole.

Melt the butter in a medium skillet over medium heat. Add the onion and celery and cook, stirring occasionally, for 7 to 8 minutes or until softened. Stir in the thyme and prosciutto.

Put the stuffing cubes in a large bowl. Add the barley, vegetable-prosciutto mixture, and broth. Toss gently until combined.

Put the dressing in the prepared casserole, cover, and bake for 45 minutes or until hot.

SOUTHERN-STYLE PEANUT AND OYSTER DRESSING

Makes about 10 cups;
not recommended as a stuffing

Southern cooking is celebrated for its magnificent flavor combinations and fine ingredients. In this recipe, we combine some of the best of the South by pairing Georgia peanuts with low-country oysters, both bound together with cornbread and good-tasting herbs.

12 tablespoons (1½ sticks) unsalted butter or margarine
1 large onion, chopped
6 stalks celery, cut into ¼-inch slices
½ pound sliced country or smoked ham, coarsely chopped
1 pint freshly shucked oysters, drained, liquor reserved
1 16-ounce package cornbread stuffing crumbs
1 8-ounce bottle clam juice
3 tablespoons cream sherry, optional
1 large egg, beaten
1½ cups dry roasted peanuts
1 bunch parsley, finely chopped
2 teaspoons dried thyme
¼ teaspoon freshly ground black pepper
Dash of ground red pepper

Preheat the oven to 325°F. Butter a shallow 3-quart casserole.

Melt the butter in a large skillet over medium-high heat. Add the onion and celery and cook, stirring occasionally, for 5 minutes. Reduce the heat to medium-low and continue cooking for 10 to 15 minutes more, until the vegetables are very soft. Add the ham and cook for 5 minutes more.

Coarsely chop the oysters. Combine the vegetable mixture, oysters, and cornbread crumbs in a large bowl. Add the clam juice to the reserved oyster liquor to make 1½ cups. Pour the clam-oyster juice and the sherry over the dressing, stirring until well moistened. Stir in the egg. Add the peanuts, parsley, thyme, and ground peppers and mix together well.

Put the dressing in the prepared casserole, cover, and bake for 45 to 60 minutes or until hot.

11

SIDE DISHES

How often have you used the phrase "turkey with all the trimmings"? And when you do, you generally mean more than turkey and stuffing. You are imagining a tantalizing array of vegetable and grain side dishes, with turkey as the star. The supporting roles are every bit as important to the success of the meal as the main part, and year after year, meal after meal, home cooks try to come up with new and fanciful ways to prepare onions, Brussels sprouts, rice, potatoes, squash, string beans, and other seasonal produce.

In this chapter, we have recipe after recipe for delicious vegetable and grain dishes that complement turkey perfectly. From a simple rice and pea casserole to a mélange of caramelized fall vegetables and a tasty barley pilaf, we have delicious answers to your menu questions. We team Brussels sprouts with chestnuts and with carrots, we stuff onions with spinach and goat cheese, and we layer white and sweet potatoes in a tempting casserole. Best of all, these dishes go far beyond the Thanksgiving and Christmas tables. They promise to become favorites for family suppers and dinner parties throughout the year.

CARAMELIZED NEW ENGLAND VEGETABLES

Serves 8 to 10

Caramelizing vegetables simply requires heating sugar until it is melted and browned and then finishing the already cooked potatoes, parsnips, turnips, and carrots in the same pan. Butter or margarine is usually added to help the sugar form a syrup and to add flavor. The hot sugar will sizzle when you add the butter and water, so be sure to stand back from the pan and use a good oven mitt. The sizzle ceases upon stirring. This traditional assortment of Thanksgiving vegetables makes a good accompaniment to the holiday turkey—a departure from the more customary caramelized onions.

6 small red potatoes, cut in half (1 to 1½ pounds)
5 small parsnips, peeled, halved lengthwise, and
    quartered crosswise (about 1 pound)
3 medium turnips, peeled and quartered (about 1
    pound)
Salt
6 small carrots, peeled, halved lengthwise, and
    quartered crosswise (about 1 pound)
½ cup sugar
4 tablespoons unsalted butter or margarine
1 teaspoon dry mustard
½ teaspoon salt
¼ cup water
12 large scallions, including tops, cut into 5-inch lengths

Put the potatoes, parsnips, and turnips in a large sauce-pan. Cover with water, add salt to taste, cover, and bring to a boil over high heat. Cook for 10 minutes. Add the carrots and cook, covered, for 8 minutes more or until the vegetables are just tender. Remove the vegetables from the heat, drain well, and set aside.

Meanwhile, put the sugar in a heavy 4-quart saucepan and heat over medium-low heat without stirring until just melting. Continue to cook, stirring, for 3 to 5 minutes or until the sugar turns golden brown. Stir in the butter, mustard, and the ½ teaspoon salt. Gradually add the water. Cook, stirring, over low heat for 4 to 6 minutes or until smooth. The mixture will be sticky and thick in places but will become smooth with cooking.

Add the drained vegetables and the scallions to the glaze. Cook, stirring, for 2 to 4 minutes or until the vegetables are glazed and heated through. Remove the vegetables with a slotted spoon and arrange on a serving platter.

MAPLE-GLAZED BRUSSELS SPROUTS AND CHESTNUTS

Serves 6 to 8

Brussels sprouts are one of the last vegetables to be harvested from the autumn garden, which means they are fresh and delicious well into the fall. Here we team them with bacon and maple syrup for a dramatic smoky-sweet flavor experience.

The chestnuts are integral to the recipe. For maximum freshness, buy them fresh, in the shells. To peel them, see page 194.

---

24 fresh chestnuts, peeled
2 cups chicken broth
6 slices bacon, diced
1½ pounds Brussels sprouts, trimmed and blanched
2½ tablespoons maple syrup
Salt
Freshly ground black pepper

Put the peeled chestnuts and chicken broth in a medium saucepan and bring to a boil over high heat. Reduce the heat to medium and simmer for 25 minutes or until the chestnuts are tender. Remove from the heat. Drain the chestnuts in a sieve, reserving 3 tablespoons of the broth. Set aside the chestnuts and broth.

Meanwhile, cook the bacon in a medium skillet until crisp. Drain on paper towels. Pour off all but 2 tablespoons of the bacon fat.

Cut the sprouts in half lengthwise and add to the reserved fat in the skillet. Add the chestnuts and reserved broth. Stir in the maple syrup and cook over medium heat, stirring frequently, for 3 minutes or until the liquid is reduced to a glazelike consistency. Add the bacon and season with salt and pepper to taste. Serve immediately.

BRUSSELS SPROUTS AND BABY CARROTS WITH ZESTY MUSTARD SAUCE

Serves 8 to 10

The easy mustard sauce here begins with a classic white sauce and as delicious as it tastes with Brussels sprouts and baby carrots, it will also liven up broccoli and cauliflower.

---

3 tablespoons unsalted butter or margarine
3 tablespoons all-purpose flour
¼ teaspoon salt
⅛ teaspoon freshly ground black pepper
2 cups milk
2 tablespoons Dijon mustard
1 teaspoon finely grated lemon or lime zest
1 tablespoon fresh lemon or lime juice
4 cups Brussels sprouts or 2 10-ounce packages frozen
    Brussels sprouts
1 pound baby or regular carrots, cut into 2-inch pieces

Melt the butter in a medium saucepan over low heat. Stir in the flour, salt, and pepper until blended. Gradually stir in the milk and cook, stirring constantly, over medium heat until thickened and bubbly. Stir in the mustard, lemon zest, and lemon juice. Continue to cook, stirring, for 1 minute more. Remove the sauce from the heat and keep warm.

Cut any large Brussels sprouts in half. Put the sprouts in a 3-quart saucepan. Add the carrots and 1 cup water. Cover and bring just to a boil over high heat. Reduce the heat and simmer, uncovered, for 15 to 20 minutes or until the vegetables are crisp-tender.

Drain the vegetables well and combine with the mustard sauce.

SPINACH AND ARTICHOKE CASSEROLE

Serves 8 to 10

Variations on this creamy, rich spinach casserole appear in nearly every Southern cookbook. Ours is extra good because of the soft crust made from sour cream and Parmesan.

¼ cup olive oil
2 cloves garlic, minced
1 bunch scallions, trimmed and finely chopped
8 ounces mushrooms, sliced
2 10-ounce packages frozen chopped spinach, thawed and well drained
2 13¾-ounce cans artichoke hearts, drained and sliced
2½ tablespoons all-purpose flour
1 cup half-and-half
½ teaspoon grated nutmeg
1 tablespoon fresh lemon juice
Salt
Freshly ground black pepper
1 cup sour cream
½ cup (2 ounces) freshly grated Parmesan cheese
Paprika, optional

Preheat the oven to 350°F. Butter a 1½- to 2-quart casserole.

Heat the olive oil in a large skillet over medium heat. Add the garlic and scallions and cook, stirring occasionally, for 2 to 3 minutes or until softened. Add the mushrooms and continue to sauté for 5 minutes. Stir in the spinach and half the sliced artichoke hearts. Cook for about 3 minutes or until heated through.

Sprinkle the flour over the ingredients in the skillet and cook, stirring constantly, for 1 minute. Slowly pour in the half-and-half and cook for 3 to 5 minutes or until thickened. Add the nutmeg and lemon juice and season with salt and pepper to taste. Turn the spinach mixture into the prepared casserole. Spread the remaining artichoke hearts over the top.

To make the topping, mix the sour cream with the Parmesan until well blended. Spread evenly over the top of the casserole. Sprinkle lightly with paprika, if desired.

Bake the casserole for 35 to 40 minutes until bubbly. Serve hot.

SAFFRON RICE AND PEAS

Serves 4 to 6

There's nothing to this quick rice casserole: Combine the ingredients and let the oven do the rest of the work. Saffron adds festive golden color, which is offset by bright, green peas.

1 cup uncooked long-grain rice
2 teaspoons chicken bouillon granules
⅛ teaspoon ground saffron
3 cups boiling water
2 cups frozen peas

Preheat the oven to 375°F. Combine all the ingredients except the peas in a casserole. Cover and bake for 20 minutes. Add the peas and bake for 10 minutes more.

CARROTS AND NEW POTATOES

Serves 4

½ pound baby or regular carrots, cut into 1-inch
    pieces
12 small new potatoes, peeled (2 to 2½ pounds)
½ teaspoon salt
2 tablespoons unsalted butter or margarine
2 tablespoons water

Preheat the oven to 400°F. Put the carrots and potatoes in a 1-quart casserole. Sprinkle with the salt, dot with the butter, and add the water. Cover and bake for 45 minutes.

LEMON-BUTTER GLAZED VEGETABLES

Serves 10 to 12

Zippy lemon-flavored butter or margarine gives these gently cooked vegetables bright flavor. The zest is the colored part of the lemon rind; be careful not to include any of the bitter white pith.

4 cups sliced carrots
4 cups cauliflower florets
4 cups broccoli florets
1 tablespoon fresh lemon juice
1 teaspoon grated lemon zest
5 tablespoons unsalted butter or margarine, melted

Bring a large saucepan of salted water to a boil over high heat. Add the carrots, reduce the heat to medium, and cook, covered, for 5 minutes. Add the cauliflower to the pan and continue to cook for 3 minutes. Add the broccoli and cook for 2 to 3 minutes more. Remove the vegetables from the heat and drain well.

Combine the lemon juice, zest, and melted butter. Toss the lemon butter with the drained hot vegetables and serve at once.

CRANBERRY-CARROT SQUASH

Serves 8

The sweet deep flavor of acorn squash tastes wonderful with roast turkey and recipes for turkey parts. Autumn and early winter are the best times to buy acorn squash, which keeps for several days stored at cool room temperature.

4 small acorn squash
2 tablespoons unsalted butter or margarine, melted
1 10-ounce package frozen cranberry with orange sauce, thawed
½ cup coarsely grated carrot
3 tablespoons packed brown sugar
¼ teaspoon ground cinnamon

Preheat the oven to 350°F.

Cut the squash in half lengthwise. Scoop out the seeds and stringy parts. If desired, cut the halves in half again crosswise. Trim the bottoms so that the squashes do not wobble in the pan. Put the pieces, cut side up, in a baking pan. Brush the cut portions of the squash halves with the melted butter and bake for 1 hour.

Meanwhile, combine the cranberry, carrot, brown sugar, and cinnamon in a small saucepan and heat over low heat.

To serve, spoon 1 to 2 tablespoons of the cranberry-carrot mixture into each piece of squash.

ACORN SQUASH, APPLE, AND ONION GRATIN

Serves 8 to 10

The flavors of acorn squash, apples, and onions kissed with a hint of maple syrup and cinnamon combine in this magnificent casserole that will fill your kitchen with its enticing aromas. We suggest Red Delicious and Granny Smith apples, but use any good, firm apples that are in season in your area.

2 medium acorn squash
1 medium Red Delicious apple
1 medium Granny Smith apple
1 medium red onion
Salt
Freshly ground black pepper
4 tablespoons unsalted butter or margarine
½ cup chicken broth
⅓ cup maple syrup
½ teaspoon ground cinnamon
1 cup (4 ounces) shredded sharp cheddar cheese

Preheat the oven to 375°F.

Cut the acorn squash in half lengthwise and scoop out the seeds and stringy parts. Cut each squash in half crosswise into ¼-inch slices. Carefully remove the peel from each slice. Arrange the squash slices, cut side down, in a 13 × 9 × 2-inch glass baking dish or shallow 2½- to 3-quart oval casserole so that they form compact rows.

Core the apples and cut them into thin wedges. Tuck the apple wedges, peel side up, randomly between the squash slices. Cut the onion in half and each half crosswise into thin slices. Tuck the onion slices randomly between the apple and squash slices. Sprinkle with salt and pepper to taste.

Combine the butter, chicken broth, maple syrup, and cinnamon in a small saucepan. Cook, stirring, over medium heat until the butter is melted. Drizzle the mixture evenly over the squash. Cover the dish tightly with aluminum foil. Bake for 30 minutes.

Remove the aluminum foil and continue to bake for 30 minutes more or until the squash is tender. Sprinkle the shredded cheese over the top and bake for 3 to 5 minutes more or until the cheese is melted. Serve immediately.

BAKED PUMPKIN CHEESE GRITS

Serves 8

For years, Southern cooks have known that cheese and grits make a great combination. Here, we take it a step further and add pumpkin purée. The result is a tender baked side dish that complements turkey to a "tee." Grits, which are made from ground corn but are not as finely ground as cornmeal, may be a staple in the South, but are sold in supermarkets from coast to coast.

2 cups chicken broth
2 cups water
1 clove garlic, minced
1 cup quick-cooking (not instant) hominy grits
1 16-ounce can unsweetened solid-pack pumpkin
2 large eggs
1½ cups (6 ounces) shredded sharp cheddar cheese
Dash of grated nutmeg
Dash of ground red pepper
Salt
Freshly ground black pepper

Preheat the oven to 350°F. Butter a 2- to 2½-quart baking dish or casserole.

Put the chicken broth, water, and garlic in a medium saucepan over high heat. Bring to a boil and slowly stir in the grits. Reduce the heat to medium-low and simmer, stirring frequently, for 7 to 10 minutes, until thickened. Add the pumpkin and stir until thoroughly combined.

Beat the eggs in a small bowl. Add a little of the hot grits to the beaten eggs. Add the mixture back to the pan and stir to combine. Add the cheese and stir until melted. Season the grits with the nutmeg and red pepper and add salt and pepper to taste. Transfer the grits to the prepared baking dish and bake for 40 to 50 minutes, until set and lightly puffed. Let stand for 5 minutes before serving.

WARM GREEN BEAN AND ONION RING SALAD

Serves 8 to 10

French fried onion rings provide crunch and zesty flavor to fresh green beans that are cooked here until crisp-tender, then dressed with a warm mustardy dressing.

1 2.8-ounce can French fried onions
2 tablespoons Dijon mustard
2 tablespoons cider vinegar
2 shallots, minced
½ cup olive oil
Salt
Freshly ground black pepper
2 pounds fresh green beans, ends trimmed

Preheat the oven to 350°F. Spread the onion rings on a baking sheet and crisp in the oven for 7 to 10 minutes. Turn the oven off and leave the onions in it to keep warm.

Put the mustard and vinegar in a small saucepan and whisk to combine. Add the shallots and slowly whisk in the olive oil. Season with salt and pepper to taste. Bring the mixture to a boil, stirring constantly, and cook for 2 minutes. Keep warm over low heat.

Cook the beans in a large pan of boiling water for 4 to 5 minutes until just crisp-tender. Drain and immediately transfer to a serving bowl. Toss with the warm dressing and stir in the toasted onion rings. Serve immediately.

WALNUT WILD RICE WITH BRUSSELS SPROUTS

Serves 10 to 12

The sweetness of Brussels sprouts is wonderful with nutty wild rice, particularly when it is further enhanced with garlic, onion, cream, and a good measure of walnuts. We use a blend of wild and long-grain white rice for this casserole, which makes it more economical and textur-ally more interesting.

4 tablespoons unsalted butter or margarine
1 cup chopped onion
2 cloves garlic, minced
4¼ cups water
2 6-ounce packages long grain and wild rice mix
2 cups trimmed Brussels sprouts, cut lengthwise into
    ¼-inch slices
½ cup heavy cream or half-and-half
½ cup chopped walnuts, lightly toasted
⅛ teaspoon grated nutmeg

Melt the butter in a large saucepan over medium heat. Add the onion and garlic and cook, stirring occasionally, until softened but not brown. Add the water, rice, and contents of the seasoning packets. Bring to a boil, cover tightly, and simmer for 20 minutes.

Stir the Brussels sprouts into the rice. Continue to simmer, covered, for about 5 minutes, or until all the liquid is absorbed. Stir in the cream, almonds, and nutmeg just before serving.

ORANGE-BARLEY PILAF

Serves 8

Barley is a grain that is easy to find in the supermarkets and often used in soups. But it is wonderful in pilafs and casseroles, too. Medium pearl barley refers to barley that has been husked, or pearled, and that cooks in a moderate amount of time rather than instantly. Some barley is labeled "fast-cooking," which means it has been presteamed during processing. In this recipe we team barley with orange juice, a novel and delicious idea. Tangerines, clementines, and mandarins, all related, are available in the greengrocers and supermarkets from December to mid-February and can be substituted in this recipe.

2 tablespoons unsalted butter or margarine
1 medium onion, chopped
1 clove garlic, minced
1 cup medium pearl barley
2¼ cups chicken broth
¼ cup dry sherry
¼ cup orange juice
2 teaspoons orange zest
½ teaspoon dried basil
½ teaspoon dried tarragon
¼ teaspoon salt
⅛ teaspoon freshly ground black pepper
½ cup coarsely grated carrot
⅓ cup chopped parsley
⅓ cup pine nuts, lightly toasted, optional

Melt the butter in a medium saucepan over medium heat. Add the onion and cook, stirring occasionally, for about 5 minutes or until softened. Stir in the garlic and barley and cook for 1 to 2 minutes more. Add the broth, sherry, orange juice and zest, basil, tarragon, salt, and pepper. Bring to a boil. Reduce the heat, cover, and simmer for about 40 minutes or until the barley is tender and the liquid is absorbed. Stir in the carrot, parsley, and pine nuts, if desired, just before serving.

GLAZED CARROT-PECAN WILD RICE

Serves 10 to 12

Orange-flavored liqueur, such as Triple Sec, Cointreau, or Grand Marnier, gives this dish the sunny taste of citrus.

4¼ cups water
4 tablespoons unsalted butter or margarine
2 6-ounce packages long grain and wild rice mix
½ cup orange-flavored liqueur
1 tablespoon packed brown sugar
⅛ teaspoon ground allspice
6 medium carrots, cut into short julienne strips
    (about 2 cups)
½ cup pecan halves or pieces, lightly toasted

Combine the water with 2 tablespoons of the butter, the rice, and contents of the seasoning packets in a large saucepan. Bring to a boil, cover tightly, and simmer for about 25 minutes or until all the liquid is absorbed.

Meanwhile, melt the remaining 2 tablespoons butter in a 10-inch skillet. Stir in the liqueur, brown sugar, allspice, and carrots. Cook, uncovered, over medium heat, stirring frequently, for 5 to 7 minutes or until the carrots are crisp-tender.

Gently stir the carrots into the hot cooked rice. Sprinkle with the pecans before serving.

PUMPKIN-SPICED
SWEET POTATO NUGGETS

Serves 8

These nut-crusted nuggets teamed with two of the best vegetables of the fall season—pumpkin and sweet potatoes—are a charming addition to the turkey platter. And they are equally good served alongside turkey parts or roast turkey breast.

3 medium sweet potatoes, cooked and peeled
1 cup canned unsweetened solid-pack pumpkin
½ teaspoon salt
½ teaspoon ground cinnamon
¼ teaspoon grated nutmeg
⅛ teaspoon ground ginger
¼ cup milk
2 cups finely chopped walnuts, pecans, or almonds, or a
    combination

Preheat the oven to 350°F.

Cut the sweet potatoes into quarters and put in a mixing bowl. Mash the potatoes with the back of a fork or a potato masher to soften. Add the pumpkin, salt and spices, and milk and stir until well blended. Using a tablespoon, shape the mixture into 1-inch round balls and roll in the chopped nuts until evenly coated. Put the balls on a baking sheet and heat in the oven for 15 to 20 minutes.

STUFFED SWEET POTATOES

Serves 8

Sweet potatoes are one of the most nutritious vegetables you can buy. Luckily they are available much of the year, but they are never better than in the autumn. Their natural sweetness makes them an obvious accompaniment to mild-tasting turkey, and dressed up a little with cheese and apples, they make a remarkable side dish. Sweet potatoes may have light-colored or dark orange flesh. If the latter, they often are labeled "yams," although botanically speaking they are not really yams. Darker potatoes, with a reddish skin, are moister than the lighter potatoes. Use either in these recipes.

8 medium sweet potatoes (2 to 3 pounds)
1 cup (4 ounces) shredded medium-sharp cheddar cheese
4 tablespoons unsalted butter or margarine, softened
1 teaspoon salt
Dash of freshly ground white pepper
8 slices bacon, cooked and crumbled
1 medium Red Delicious apple, peeled, cored, and finely chopped

Preheat the oven to 350°F.

Wash the potatoes, prick with the tines of a fork, and bake for 1 hour or until tender. Cut a slice off the wide top of each potato. Scoop out the cooked potato, being careful not to break the skin. Leave an ⅛-inch shell. Set the shells aside.

Mash the scooped-out potato with the cheese, butter, salt, and pepper in a medium bowl. Fold in the bacon and apple. Spoon the mixture into the potato shells and put in a baking dish large enough to hold the potatoes. Bake for 25 to 30 minutes until hot.

MAPLE-GLAZED SWEET POTATOES

Serves 6 to 8

Despite its sweetness, maple syrup only makes sweet potatoes taste better, but never cloyingly sweet.

½ cup fresh orange juice
1 tablespoon cornstarch
3 tablespoons unsalted butter or margarine
½ cup maple syrup
1 teaspoon grated orange zest
4 medium sweet potatoes, cooked, peeled, and
    quartered (about 1½ pounds)

Combine the orange juice with the cornstarch in a small bowl and stir until blended.

Melt the butter in a large skillet over medium heat. Add the orange juice mixture, maple syrup, and orange zest. Cook, stirring, until the glaze is thickened and clear. Add the cooked sweet potatoes and heat through. Serve at once.

APRICOT AND PECAN
SWEET POTATOES

Serves 8

Sweet potatoes marry well with fruity flavors and here we combine them with apricot preserves and apricot brandy in an easy casserole.

4 medium sweet potatoes, cooked and peeled
  (about 1½ pounds)
½ cup apricot preserves
¼ cup apricot brandy or schnapps
2 tablespoons unsalted butter or margarine
¼ cup coarsely chopped pecans

Preheat the oven to 325°F. Lightly butter a shallow 1½-quart baking dish. Cut the potatoes into pieces and put them in the prepared baking dish.

Combine the preserves, brandy, and butter in a small saucepan and simmer over medium heat for 3 to 4 minutes. Spoon the mixture over the potatoes and sprinkle with the pecans. Bake for 30 minutes or until hot and bubbly.

OVEN-BAKED POTATOES AND PARSNIPS

Serves 12

You may not have considered combining potatoes and parsnips in quite this way, but the hint of garlic and the mildness of the Swiss cheese give them the flavor boost and texture they need to make a winning pair.

---

1 clove garlic
8 medium baking potatoes, such as russets, peeled and
    thinly sliced (about 3 pounds)
1 teaspoon dried thyme
Salt
Freshly ground black pepper
8 small parsnips, peeled and thinly sliced
    (about 1½ pounds)
1½ cups (6 ounces) shredded Swiss cheese
2½ cups half-and-half

Preheat the oven to 350°F. Generously butter a 13 × 9 × 2-inch casserole. Cut the garlic clove in half and rub the halves over the inside of the buttered casserole.

Spread a third of the potato slices in the casserole. Season with a little thyme, salt, and pepper. Cover with a third of the sliced parsnips and top with about a third of the shredded cheese. Repeat layering and seasoning until all the vegetables and cheese are used.

Pour the half-and-half evenly over the vegetables in the casserole. Cover the casserole with aluminum foil and bake for 30 minutes. Remove the foil and bake for an additional 40 to 50 minutes or until the gratin is crisp and golden on top. Let the gratin stand for a few minutes before serving.

TWO POTATO BAKE

Serves 10 to 12

If you are accustomed to preparing both white and sweet potatoes for Thanksgiving dinner, give yourself a break. This delicious alternative calls for both potatoes—and best of all, you can cook it alongside the turkey if the oven is large enough.

4 large baking potatoes, such as russets, peeled and thinly sliced (2½ to 3 pounds)
2 large sweet potatoes, peeled and thinly sliced (1 to 1½ pounds)
2 medium carrots, cut into fine julienne strips
⅔ cup finely chopped scallions
½ teaspoon dried rosemary, crushed, or 1½ teaspoons finely chopped fresh
1 teaspoon chicken bouillon granules
½ cup hot water
4 tablespoons unsalted butter or margarine, melted
Chopped scallions, optional

Preheat the oven to 325°F. Lightly butter a 12 × 8-inch baking dish.

Put the white potato slices in a bowl of ice water for at least 5 minutes to prevent discoloration and to crisp them. Drain well. Put the sweet potato slices in another bowl of cold water for 5 minutes, then drain well.

Spread half the white potato slices in the prepared baking dish. Sprinkle with half the carrots and scallions and a third of the rosemary. Top with the sweet potato slices. Sprinkle with the remaining carrots and scallions and half the remaining rosemary. Top with the remaining white potatoes and rosemary.

Dissolve the bouillon granules in the hot water and pour over the potatoes. Cover the dish with aluminum foil and bake for 1¼ to 1½ hours or until the potatoes are just tender. Remove the foil. Drizzle the melted butter over the potatoes and bake, uncovered, for 20 to 25 minutes more or until the potatoes are tender. Garnish with additional chopped scallions before serving.

HASH BROWN POTATO CASSEROLE

Serves 8 to 12

If your family loves hash browns, do not relegate them to the weekend breakfast table. With a few packages of frozen hash browns in the freezer, you can quickly concoct a bubbling, cheesy casserole fit for breakfast, lunch, or dinner

2 pounds frozen hash brown potatoes, thawed
2 cups (8 ounces) shredded sharp cheddar cheese
2 cups sour cream
1 10¾-ounce can cream of chicken soup
⅔ cup chopped onion
10 tablespoons (⅔ cup) unsalted butter or margarine, melted
¾ teaspoon salt
¼ teaspoon freshly ground black pepper
2 cups cornflakes, crushed

Preheat the oven to 350°F. Lightly butter a shallow 3-quart baking dish.

Put the thawed potatoes, cheese, sour cream, soup, onion, 5 tablespoons of the butter, salt, and pepper in a large bowl and stir to combine. Pour the mixture into the prepared baking dish.

Combine the remaining 5 tablespoons butter with the cornflakes in a small bowl and sprinkle over the potatoes. Bake for 40 to 50 minutes or until hot and bubbly. Let stand for 10 minutes before serving.

GOLDEN MASHED POTATOES

Serves 4 to 5

The carrots give these mashed potatoes special flavor and making them with nonfat dry milk removes some of the calories associated with conventional mashed potatoes—without robbing them of taste, creaminess, or richness.

4 medium baking potatoes, such as russets, peeled and
    cut into pieces (about 1 pound)
1½ cups water
½ teaspoon salt
3 tablespoons unsalted butter or margarine
¼ cup nonfat dry milk
½ cup grated carrot
Salt
Freshly ground black pepper

Preheat the oven to 375°F. Lightly butter a 1-quart casserole.

Put the potatoes in a large saucepan and add the water and the ½ teaspoon salt. Bring to a boil over high heat and cook, covered, over medium heat for about 15 minutes or until tender. Drain the potatoes, reserving the water.

Mash the potatoes with 2 tablespoons of the butter and the milk. Gradually stir in the reserved cooking water until the desired consistency is achieved. Fold in the carrot and season with salt and pepper to taste.

Put the potato mixture in the prepared casserole and top with the remaining tablespoon butter. Bake for 20 to 30 minutes or until hot and lightly browned.

12

SAUCES, RELISHES, CHUTNEYS, COMPOTES, AND GRAVIES

Does the gravy disappear before the gravy boat makes it once around the table? Are there heated family debates every year about what sort of cranberry sauce is best? Just about everyone, it seems, has strong feelings about the condiments that round out a turkey meal—and there is never enough gravy. In this chapter, we come to the rescue with a number of recipes for chunky sauces, fruity compotes, tangy chutneys, and rich gravies guaranteed to keep everyone happy as the meal progresses. And as good as these accompaniments are on the holiday table, they will add that special something to every turkey meal year round.

WHOLE CRANBERRY SAUCE WITH PORT AND PECANS

Makes about 4 cups

For those who like cooked cranberry sauce, this mixture of fresh berries, dried apricots, and the crunch of pecans is bound to please.

4 cups fresh cranberries (about 1 pound)
1 cup dried apricots, chopped
¾ cup sugar
½ cup port wine or cranberry juice cocktail
½ cup fresh orange juice
½ cup packed brown sugar
¾ cup pecan halves, lightly toasted

In a large saucepan, combine the cranberries, apricots, sugar, port, orange juice, and brown sugar. Cook over medium heat, stirring occasionally, for 25 to 30 minutes or until the sauce thickens to the desired consistency. Remove from the heat and let cool. Stir in the pecans.

Pour the sauce into an airtight container. Cover and store in the refrigerator. Bring the sauce to room temperature before serving. The sauce may be stored in the refrigerator for up to 2 weeks.

CRANBERRY CHUTNEY

Makes 2 cups

Here is another type of cooked cranberry sauce—this one flavored with green bell peppers and mustard. Try it on turkey sandwiches

2 cups fresh cranberries, chopped (about ½ pound)
1 medium onion, chopped
½ medium green bell pepper, chopped
½ cup sugar
¼ cup Dijon mustard

Combine all the ingredients in a medium saucepan. Simmer, uncovered, for 10 minutes or until the cranberries are tender, stirring occasionally.

Chill the chutney before serving. The chutney may be stored in the refrigerator in a covered container for 2 days.

CRANBERRY COMPOTE

Makes 2 cups

This fruit compote of assorted fresh fruits and raisins is best when allowed to "age" overnight or longer. Try it with leftover cold turkey or to dress up roast turkey breast or grilled turkey parts.

1 tablespoon unsalted butter or margarine
2 tablespoons chopped onion
1 cup fresh or frozen cranberries (about 4 ounces)
¼ cup chopped apple
¼ cup firmly packed brown sugar
½ cup apple juice
¼ cup raisins
¼ cup chopped orange segments
1 teaspoon grated orange zest
⅛ teaspoon ground cinnamon

Melt the butter in a medium saucepan over medium heat. Add the onion and cook, stirring occasionally, for about 5 minutes or until softened. Add the cranberries, apple, sugar, and apple juice and bring to a boil. Reduce the heat and simmer for 4 to 5 minutes or until the fruit has softened. Remove from the heat and stir in the raisins, orange segments, orange zest, and cinnamon.

Let the compote stand for 1 to 2 hours or refrigerate, covered, overnight.

WARM CHERRY CHUTNEY

Makes 1¾ cups

Try sweet dark cherries as the base for chutney for a pleasant change from cranberries.

---

1 16-ounce can pitted dark sweet cherries, packed in syrup
1 tablespoon unsalted butter or margarine
½ cup chopped onion
1 clove garlic, minced
2 tablespoons cider vinegar
2 tablespoons sugar
1 tablespoon cornstarch
1½ teaspoons curry powder
½ teaspoon ground ginger
Salt

Drain the cherries, reserving ½ cup of the syrup. Chop the cherries into small pieces and set aside.

Melt the butter in a small saucepan over medium heat. Add the onion and garlic and cook, stirring occasionally, for 4 minutes or until softened. Remove the pan from the heat. Add the reserved syrup and the vinegar to the pan.

In a small bowl, stir together the sugar, cornstarch, curry powder, ginger, and salt to taste. Gradually stir the sugar mixture into the onion mixture. Cook over medium heat, stirring, until the sauce thickens and bubbles. Add the chopped cherries. Reduce the heat and simmer for 3 to 5 minutes to blend the flavors. Store in a covered container in the refrigerator for up to 3 days.

SHERRY AND TURKEY GIBLET GRAVY

Makes about 4 cups

Only attempt this rich gravy when you are roasting a turkey, as the pan drippings are integral to the outcome of the recipe.

1 12-pound fresh or frozen Butterball turkey
5 cups water
1 small onion, peeled and cut into quarters
1 bay leaf
½ teaspoon dried thyme, crushed
½ cup medium dry sherry or chicken broth
3 tablespoons all-purpose flour
2 tablespoons soy sauce
Freshly ground black pepper
⅓ cup heavy cream

Prepare the turkey for roasting according to package directions or follow the directions on pages 8–11. Put the turkey neck, heart, and gizzard in a medium saucepan with the water. Add the onion, bay leaf, and thyme. Bring to a boil and simmer, partially covered, for 1½ hours. Add the liver to the saucepan and simmer for 30 minutes more. Strain the broth into a bowl, reserving the giblets. You should have about 2½ cups. Set the broth aside. Discard the neck. Finely chop the giblets and set aside.

When the turkey is done, skim the fat from the drippings, using a turkey baster or skimming spoon. Put 3 tablespoons fat in a saucepan. Discard the remaining fat. Add the sherry to the drippings remaining in the roasting pan and set it over medium-high heat. Bring the liquid to a boil, scraping any brown bits from the bottom of the pan. Reduce the heat and simmer for 5 minutes. Remove from the heat.

Add the flour to the fat in the saucepan, stirring until smooth. Cook, stirring, over medium heat for 2 minutes. Gradually stir in the reserved giblet broth, together with the roasting pan juices. Bring to a boil, reduce the heat, and simmer for 3 to 5 minutes more or until the gravy is thickened and bubbly. Add the soy sauce and pepper to taste. Stir in the chopped giblets and cream.

Serve the gravy with the roasted Butterball turkey.

TRADITIONAL COUNTRY KITCHEN GRAVY

Makes about 4 cups

Similar to the sherry and giblet gravy, this one is best made with Turkey Frame Broth (page 146) that you have prepared at an earlier time from another turkey and kept frozen for gravy or soup. Like the sherry and giblet gravy, this recipe relies on the pan drippings from a roast turkey, so plan to serve it when you are roasting a whole bird or a turkey breast.

Turkey fat and drippings from roasting pan
About 3 cups Turkey Frame Broth (page 146) or Giblet
    Broth (recipe follows)
½ cup flour
Salt
Freshly ground black pepper
Cooked giblets, finely chopped, optional
½ cup sour cream, optional
2 tablespoons chopped parsley, optional
1 2½-ounce jar sliced mushrooms, drained, optional

Remove the fat from the roasting pan, using a turkey baster or skimming spoon. Put 4 tablespoons of fat in a saucepan and discard the rest.

Pour the drippings from the turkey roasting pan into a large measuring cup. Add enough broth to the drippings to make 4 cups.

Stir the flour into the fat in the saucepan. Gradually blend the drippings into the flour mixture. Bring to a boil, stirring constantly. Continue to cook for 3 to 5 minutes, until the gravy is thickened. Season with salt and pepper to taste. Add the chopped cooked giblets and one of the other optional additions, if desired.

GIBLET BROTH

Makes about 3 cups

Use this to flavor gravy (pages 254 and 256). It freezes well and you will want to keep some on hand to enhance gravies and stuffings.

Neck, heart, gizzard, and liver of 1 Butterball turkey
5 cups water
2 teaspoons salt

Put the neck, heart, and gizzard in a large heavy saucepan. Add the water and salt and bring to a boil over high heat. Lower the heat and simmer, partially covered, for 2 hours. Add the liver and simmer for 30 minutes more.

Strain the broth. Chop the giblets to use in gravy or stuffing.

APPLE-CINNAMON SAUCE

Makes 2 cups

Redolent with the flavors of autumn, this sauce will turn slices of warmed turkey into a satisfying special supper. Serve this sauce with Turkey with Apple-Pear Dressing (page 78).

1 tablespoon unsalted butter
1 teaspoon chicken bouillon granules
2 tablespoons cornstarch
1½ teaspoons sugar
½ teaspoon ground cinnamon
2 cups apple juice

Melt the butter in a medium saucepan over medium heat until light brown and bubbly. Meanwhile, combine the bouillon, cornstarch, sugar, and cinnamon in a medium bowl. Gradually blend in the apple juice.

Add the apple juice mixture to the browned butter in the pan. Cook, stirring, over medium heat until thickened. Serve over sliced turkey.

SPICY BARBECUE SAUCE

Makes about 1½ cups

This is a tangy barbecue sauce for brushing on turkey as it finishes cooking. Pass what remains at the table.

1 cup ketchup
½ cup water
¼ cup finely chopped onion
2 tablespoons sugar
2 tablespoons Worcestershire sauce
1 tablespoon vinegar
1 teaspoon salt
1 teaspoon chili powder
¼ to ½ teaspoon freshly ground black pepper

Combine all the ingredients in a medium saucepan over medium heat and bring to a boil. Reduce the heat to low and simmer for 15 minutes, stirring occasionally.

Use the sauce to baste roast turkey or turkey pieces several times during the last half hour of cooking or grilling.

INDEX

-stuffed turkey breast with
asparagus, 74–75
whole cranberry sauce with
port and, 250
Pepper:
bell, and cilantro dressing,
206–207
chili, and garlic stuffing,
turkey with, 46–47
mixed, sauté, turkey cutlets
with, 100
-sausage-pasta toss, 184–185
Pilaf, orange-barley, 234–235
Pineapple relish, grilled turkey
breast with, 76–77
Pizza(s):
franks, 183
Mexican turkey mini,
122–123
turkey calzones, 116–117
turkey pita, 176
Potato(es):
golden mashed, 247
hash brown, casserole, 246
new, carrots, and, 225
oven-baked parsnips and,
242–243
turkey salad, French, 167
two potato bake, 244–245
Pot pie:
turkey, 136–137
turkey sausage, 186–187
Prosciutto and barley dressing,
211
Pumpkin:
cheese grits, baked, 230–231
spiced sweet potato nuggets,
237
wild rice turkey soup, 150

Raisin-apple herb stuffing,
turkey with, 48–49
Raspberry-mint:
glaze, breast of turkey with,
83

sauce, turkey chops with,
101
Rice:
primavera dressing, 210
saffron peas and, 224
sweet-and-sour turkey on,
135
turkey and sausage gumbo,
148–149
turkey skillet, quick,
102–103
see also Wild rice
Rosemary-lemon turkey piccata,
93

Saffron rice and peas, 224
Sage mushroom stuffing,
194–195
Salsa, tomato-jícama, 80–81
Satay, turkey, 129
Sauerkraut, turkey with apples
and, 66–67
Sausage:
apple dressing, turkey breast
with, 82
Brown 'N Serve, stuffing,
200
cornbread, and cranberry
stuffing, 196–197
cranberry stuffing, turkey
with, 50–51
and orange cornbread
stuffing, turkey with,
44–45
and turkey gumbo, 148–
149
wild rice, and oyster
dressing, 208–209
Scallopini, turkey, 92
Sour cream, turkey breast
cutlets with tomatoes
and, 98
Spinach and artichoke
casserole, 222–223
Spoon bread, turkey, 138–139